MW00883519

Have You Ever Tried to Sell a Diamond?

AND OTHER

INVESTIGATIONS OF THE DIAMOND TRADE

By Edward Jay Epstein

A Short-Form Book

Published by FastTrack Press/ EJE Publications
Ltd. New York, New York
Copyright © by EJE Publication 2011, 2013 All Rights Reserved
ISBN-13: 978-1494372217
ISBN-10: 1494372215

Book Design and Photography by Ines and Ena Talakic
www.inesandena.com
On cover Ena Talakic

Revised, December 2013

Parts of this book appeared in The Atlantic, the Sunday Times (London),
The International Herald Tribune and The Rise and Fall of Diamonds.

For Jimmy Goldsmith

CONTENTS

Prologue

I decided I needed a vacation after finishing the publicity tour for *Legend: the Secret World of Lee Harvey Oswald* in May 1978. I rented the same house in Gassin overlooking St. Tropez in which I had learned the previous summer from former CIA officers about KGB deception. Now I wanted to find a new subject for a book that did not involve double agents, dangles, false flags, and organized deception.

When I arrived at the house that Friday night, I found it was still occupied due to a scheduling mix-up. The owner Donatella Coxen had understood that I was arriving after not before the weekend and had invited two of her English friends, Ben and Jacqueline Bonas, to spend that weekend in the house. I was about to go to the local hotel but since there was a spare bedroom, Ben Bonas graciously suggested that I join them for the week-end in the house. They both proved to be immensely enjoyable company. Ben told me he was a broker in the diamond business who represented a single client, the Diamond Trading Company in London. It was a subsidiary of the Anglo-American corporation, a South African mining giant, which in turn controlled the De Beers diamond cartel.

Over lunch I asked Bonas about the role of a broker. He explained that De Beers controlled most of the diamonds mined in the world but it did not sell directly to cutters, dealers, wholesalers or retail stores. So anyone who wanted to buy uncut diamonds first needed to find a broker with an arrangement with De Beer's Diamond Trading Company. The broker would then buy the client's diamonds for its own account, and simultaneously resell them to the client.

"Could a client select any types of diamonds he wanted?" I asked.

"Not exactly," Bonas answered. He said the broker took the client to a "sight" that occurred twice a year in the offices at the Diamond Trading Company, where the client was shown a box of diamonds of different sizes, colors, and quantities that had been specifically selected for him by the cartel. The price was also set by the cartel.
"Can a client bargain?" I asked.

"There are no negotiations at all," he answered. "The client either accepts it or rejects the box."

"So there is a choice?" I asked.

"A client rarely rejects the box," Bonas said. If he does, it is unlikely he ever will be invited to another sight or have access to De Beer's diamonds."

It was a convoluted way for a cartel to distribute its product. I asked: "Why didn't De Beers deal directly with the buyers instead of using brokers?"

"There is a bit of a problem with anti-trust laws in America." Bonas explained that the US Justice Department had been investigating De Beers' cartel activities for decades, but it was making little progress in subpoenaing its records because technically De Beers did not do business in the US. On paper at least, American diamond buyers did business with independent brokers in London, not De Beers. The broker system, even if it was no more than a fig leaf, provided legal cover for De Beer's control of the market.

"How many brokers are there?" I asked.

Bonas answered, "Not many." He added that the two principal brokers for De Beers were himself and I. Hennig, which was a subsidiary of the Hambros Bank.

"So you handle one-half the world's diamond transactions?

"It's closer to one-third," he answered.

September 20, 1978
NEW YORK

Robert Asahina invited me to lunch at the Italian Pavilion, a literary dining place on West 55th Street. He had been my editor at the Public Interest and he was now the deputy editor of the American edition of *Geo*, a German-owned upscale version of the *National Geographic*. The US edition was still in the planning stage, but the latest German edition, which Asahina handed me at lunch, was artistically designed and illustrated with eye-catching photographs. The editor-in-chief was Harold "Cappy" Kaplan. Asahina, who I greatly admired for his meticulous work at the Public Interest, told me that "Cappy" wanted a long report on the mining of diamonds, with the idea that these mines and the diamonds they produced would offer the opportunity for opulent photographs. He said that if I would agree to write the story, *Geo* would finance a trip to the world's diamond mines, and also provide me with a researcher. I thought back to my lunch with Ben Bonas in Gassin, and the well-organized diamond cartel he had so lucidly described, and the prospect of a trip to South Africa. I accepted the assignment.

October 12, 1978

Since *Geo* was paying the bill, I hired on the recommendation of a friend Marjorie Kaplan as my research assistant. She had just graduated Brown and, arriving at my home-office for her first day of work, she handed me a carefully-wrapped package. It contained about a dozen manila folders.

"Is this a present?" I asked.

"They were given to me by a friend working as a temp at an ad agency," she replied. "When she heard that I was working on this project, she copied a few files she thought might be helpful."

The files were from N.W. Ayer, which was De Beer's long-time advertising agency in the United States. They contained not only reviews of the success of past advertising campaigns, but voluminous memos outlining De Beers' strategic goals in shaping the public's perception of diamonds.

November 28, 1978
LONDON, GREAT BRITAIN

Geo, which was more than generous with expenses, booked me a first-class flight on British Air for my eight-week trip to Africa. There was first a brief stop in London. I went directly to the Diamond Trading Corporation's headquarters at Number 2 Charterhouse Street, the venue for its diamond "sights," to meet with Richard Dickson, the public relations officer in charge of visiting journalists. He was very good at his job, lucidly briefing me over tea about the extraordinary work by De Beers in discovering and mining diamonds. He assumed that I was writing the usual story to accompany photographs about the value of diamonds, and I did not disabuse him of this assumption since I needed De Beers' help in getting access to the diamond mines. I also didn't press him about the issue of how De Beers restricted the global supply since Ben Bonas had told me that De Beers had a very effective way of managing its PR machine: it kept secret from its press officers any information it did not want them to relay to journalists. "It's no use trying to wheedle anything out of them," Bonas had told me, "They don't know anything." After Dickson had taken me on a tour of the facilities, I returned to the airport to catch a direct flight to Johannesburg, South Africa.

December 4, 1978
JOHANNESBURG, SOUTH AFRICA

I met Harry Frederick Oppenheimer, the chairman of both De Beers and its parent, the Anglo-American Corporation, at 44 Main Street, a block-long building, with its imposing neo-colonial facade and marble entranceway, in the center of Johannesburg. It looked more like a government institution than the headquarters of the mining company. Once inside the well-guarded executive floor of the Anglo-American Corporation, I was taken to his office by Hank Slack, his 28-year old executive assistant. Sitting across the desk from Oppenheimer, it was hard to imagine that this small, shy man not only ran a global mining empire but controlled the world's diamond supply. He spoke quietly, but with great precision. He had a distinct Oxford accent, and as he explained an issue he tended to punctuate his answers with a self-effacing, smile. He was far more candid in discussing his business than I would have expected someone in this position to be, and I assumed that this disarming openness proceeded from his confidence in his control over his immediate universe.

When I asked him about his holdings in Africa, he said matter-of-factly that his businesses accounted for over half of the industrial exports of southern Africa.

"And the diamonds?" I asked.

"It is no secret that we acquire most of the world's available uncut diamonds." He explained that this included the production of the Soviet Union. "We have of course no reason for concealing this arrangement other than the Russians prefer not to receive any public attention for obvious reasons," he said almost apologetically. The "obvious reasons" for obscuring the arrangement with De Beers were that the Soviet Union had for some fifteen years called for a total boycott of South Africa and South African businesses, and its dealings with De Beers, if made public, might prove embarrassing.

"But how long could such an unholy alliance last?" I asked.

"As long as the Soviets want access to the diamond market," he replied. "We paid the Soviet Union more than half a billion dollars last year," he continued. "This is not a sum it can easily replace, and I can see no conceivable reason why it would want to abandon such a profitable arrangement." His logic was brutally direct: De Beers provided the Soviet Union with its single largest source of hard currency. If the Soviet Union withdrew its diamonds from De Beers, it would have to find other outlets to sell its uncut diamonds. And if it precariously dumped these diamonds on the market, the price would collapse, and the Soviet Union would lose an important source of foreign exchange. "What could the Russians possibly gain by competing with us?" He asked rhetorically.

He further pointed out that De Beers provided the Soviets with certain types of industrial diamonds that were important for drilling and producing electronic wiring. Its Siberian mines apparently did not produce these strategically important diamonds. By selling gem stones to De Beers, the Soviet Union received the credits for importing the industrial diamonds it needed.

The Soviet Union also had considerable influence in other diamond producing areas in Black Africa, such as Angola. I asked if the logic of the arrangement between De Beers and the Soviets required the Soviets to use their power in those countries to help De Beers retain its control over diamond mines there.

"You will have to address that question to the Africans concerned," he replied abruptly. The tone in his voice made it clear that there were aspects to the Soviet arrangement that he decidedly did not want to discuss.

I asked him about the situation in Namibia, De Beer's richest source of gem diamonds. Technically, Namibia was a United Nations trusteeship. In fact, however, South Africa administered this diamond-producing territory as if it were a province of that country. This had led to a potentially explosive situation. The United Nations had demanded that South Africa recognize SWAPO, the group battling for independence, and hold elections under the auspices of the UN. If South Africa failed to comply with this ultimatum, the UN threatened to impose economic sanctions, including possibly an oil embargo. To buy time, South Africa had decided to stage its own election in Namibia excluding SWAPO. Since this election would not lead to a change in the status of Namibia, it was condemned by SWAPO as a "charade."

"What the South African government hopes to accomplish by this exercise is beyond me," Oppenheimer said. "It will only delay the inevitable movement toward independence in Namibia."

"Would an independent Namibia pose a threat to De Beers' control?" I asked.

"We are prepared to deal with any legitimate government that comes to power there," he replied. "We now pay about $80 million a year in taxes on those diamonds, and that provides the territory with most of its revenues," he explained, and then added, "Whatever government eventually comes to power they will need this revenue to survive." His point was clear: Namibia needed De Beers' money as much as De Beers needed Namibia's diamonds. He was confident that SWAPO, or any other group in Namibia, would accept this bargain.

"How badly would en embargo hurt your diamond business?" I asked because the United Nations was considering imposing economic sanctions against South Africa.

"I can think of no commodity less susceptible to dangers from UN sanctions than diamonds," he said. He was stating the obvious: diamonds were after all one of the most convenient commodities to transport across borders. For example, an entire month of production of diamonds from the Namibian mines, worth $40 million, could be smuggled out of Namibia in an attaché case.

Even though I knew Oppenheimer was himself on record as opposing South Africa's policy of apartheid, South Africa was now considered a pariah nation in most of Black Africa. I asked how De Beers could continue to operate under these circumstances.

Oppenheimer said the arrangement between De Beers and Black African nations would continue because it was "mutually advantageous." He pointed out that De Beers was developing vast new mines in the Botswana desert. "These Botswana mines would provide the world with an ample supply of diamonds." Even so, he added "We are, and will remain, a South African company."

He suggested that I see for myself how De Beers operated outside of South Africa and he offered to provide me air transportation in his company's planes to visit the mines in Botswana, Lesotho and other independent nations.

After I accepted his offer, he invited me to dine in the executive dining room. The lunch began with an English butler serving gin and tonic drinks. We sat at a table with fine china and crystal glasses, which were constantly filled with vintage claret by servers. Meanwhile, a tall African chef, standing at a side board, carved roast beef. After the meal Cuban cigars were passed around the table. By the time lunch ended and I had finished my cigar, one of Oppenheimer's assistants came to the table and handed me an envelope. It contained an invitation to visit Oppenheimer's private Mala-Mala game preserve and my itinerary, including a flight the next morning to the new diamond Orapa mine in Botswana.

December 5, 1978
BOTSWANA

The small Cessna Air King took off from Jan Smuts in Johannesburg promptly at 7 A.M. for the two-hour flight to the Orapa mine. On board the plane with me were four De Beers' engineers who called themselves "the flying circus." Their job was to periodically inspect and evaluate the operations at all of De Beers' diamond mines, and then report back to Oppenheimer's headquarters in Johannesburg.

We flew directly over the eastern edge of the Kalahari Desert, which cut through Botswana in a swath of brown barren earth. There were few signs of life anywhere below except for scattered clumps of twist-ed thorn trees and an occasional herd of Oryx. By 9 A.M. the sun, was baking down on the parched earth which was partially concealed by a nimbus of dust. Suddenly, appearing like some desert mirage out of this haze was a modern city. "Orapa," the pilot announced, as he began circling for a landing.

Except for the fact that Orapa is in the middle of nowhere, it might have been any suburban city. I could see ranch houses with green lawns and rectangular swimming pools laid out along a cross-grid of paved streets. There were also a shopping center, football fields, parks and high rise apartment houses.

One journalistic advantage in flying to the diamond mines on De Beers' airplanes was that I had the opportunity to meet en route a number of consulting engineers. Seated next to me was Kenneth J. Trueman, a South African engineer working for De Beers. He ex-plained that most of the city of Orapa had in fact been prefabricated in Johannesburg in 1971, and then, piece by piece, reassembled on this stretch of desert. It had been an enormous undertaking. A road had to be bulldozed through the trackless wasteland so that trucks could move the mining equipment in, an artificial lake and a pipeline had to be constructed to bring water into Orapa, power lines had to be strung some 160 miles to the South African border, and an airstrip had to be built so that diamonds could be flown out. "This was the first mine DeBeers ever developed outside of South Africa," he con-tinued.

At the Orapa airstrip, it took only a moment to go through Botswa-na customs. Oppenheimer's headquarters had telexed ahead that I was arriving, and I was immediately issued a red badge. Without such a badge, not even a citizen of Botswana is allowed into Orapa. I re-marked to Trueman how quickly we were admitted into Botswana, considering that we did not have visas and that he was a South Afri-can citizen.

"No problem," he laughed, "Harry Oppenheimer owns Botswana lock, stock and barrel." I later found out that he wasn't far wrong. Botswana, a republic with some 6 million citizens, most nomadic tribesmen, derives more than 50 percent of its national income from diamond, manganese and copper mines controlled by Harry Oppen-heimer. The Botswana government is dependent on these mines for almost all its revenues and foreign exchange.

Jim Gibson, a lanky Scotsman in his early forties, met me at the airport. He was De Beers' chief geologist at Orapa, and he had been asked to show me around the mine. He explained as we drove back to Orapa that he had been at the mine since it went into production in 1971. When we arrived at the mine, he handed me a steel helmet. As a safety regulation, De Beers requires that everyone wear one at all its mines. "You're looking at the second largest diamond mine in the world," Gibson said, pointing to a long, oval-shaped depression in front of us. (The largest was the De Beers mine in Tanzania.)

I had imagined a mine deep underground honeycombed with labyrinthine tunnels. Instead I saw an open pit that looked like an excavation site for a skyscraper. A number of dirt roads wound their way down to the bottom of the pit, which was no more than 690 feet below the surface of the earth at its deepest point. On the floor of the mine I could see about fifty Botswana workers. They were dressed in khaki jumpsuits and yellow helmets, and most of them were operating steam shovels and other mechanized equipment.

Every few minutes, a large yellow truck driven by a Botswanan would drive down the winding road to the bottom of the mine. A power shovel would then load it with a pile of bluish earth. When the truck returned to the surface, it would dump the bluish earth on a moving conveyor belt. The entire process was highly mechanized and required relatively few workers.

"It is simply an earth-moving operation," Gibson explained. "Every afternoon at 4 P.M., a number of dynamite charges are detonated to loosen up the ground, and then the power shovels simply scoop up the kimberlite."

Kimberlite is the blue ore in the mine. "What you are looking down into is a kimberlite pipe. If all the kimberlite was scooped out of that pit, it would look something like this." He drew a sketch in the ground of something that looked like a funnel with an extremely long stem. "Millions of years ago there were underground explosions that sent lava shooting up to the surface. When the lava cooled, it hardened into this pipe like formation." The kimberlite, containing the diamonds, had come gushing up with the lava.

I picked up a handful of the kimberlite ore and crumbled it into a loose mixture of stones and bluish dust. "Where are the diamonds?" I asked.

"Finding a diamond in kimberlite is like finding a very small needle in a haystack," he responded. It is necessary to slit through more than two tons of kimberlite to find just one carat of diamonds.

A carat is a very minute measure. It is based on the remarkably uniform weight of the ancient carob seed, and weighs only 1/2000th of a pound. Separating the diamonds from this mass of bluish ore seemed a herculean task. I asked Gibson who separated out the diamonds.

"The diamonds are never touched by a human hand," he explained, as we walked along a path parallel to the conveyor belt toward a glimmering structure about one-quarter of a mile away. "That's the separation plant," he said, pointing to the building ahead. It towered about twenty stories above the desert and looked like some medieval fortress. As we approached it, I could see that it was constructed of giant slabs of metal and surrounded by a barbwire fence.

I had heard stories about natives stealing diamonds from mines by concealing them on their bodies. I wondered whether this fortress-like building was part of some draconian security system. I inquired whether they conducted body searches.

Gibson replied that there was no need for anything like that. He explained that the fully automated sorting machines kept the diamonds from tempting anyone.

The conveyor belt carries about one thousand tons of ore an hour into a plant. Inside the separation plant, the conveyor belt dumps the ore between two giant wheels-the "crushers" - which are large enough to pulverize automobiles. The kimberlite must be broken into small fragments in order to be automatically processed. The tiny particles, mainly sand, are screened out by a series of sieves. The kimberlite then moves on a conveyor belt into huge vats of swirling liquid that resemble enormous whirlpool baths. These "cyclone baths" were designed by De Beers to take advantage of the heavy density of diamonds in separating them out from lighter-density materials. Gibson explained, "They work on the same centrifugal principle as dairy creamers: at high speeds, lighter materials rise and are skimmed off."

More than 99 percent of the ore is removed in the vats; what remains is a concentrate of diamonds and other heavy minerals.

Back on the conveyor belt, the concentrate is channeled into a battery of large, five-foot-high black boxes called "sortexes." These machines take advantage of one of the natural characteristics of diamonds: the fact that they, unlike most minerals, phosphoresce under X-rays. As the concentrate passed, the machines bombarded it with X-rays. Whenever a diamond passes through, it glimmers, activating a photoelectric cell inside the sortex. The photoelectric triggers a jet of air that blows the diamond and the stones on either side of it off the conveyor belt and down a chute that leads to the sorting room.

We went next to the sorting room, which is the most heavily guarded inner sanctum in the entire diamond mining complex. Three different guards were required to put their keys into separate locks before the door could be opened. The windowless room had in its center a row of large glass boxes, which were all connected by pipes to the ceiling. "Not even the sorters have the opportunity to lay a hand on the diamonds in this system," Gibson explained.

On closer inspection, I could see that each box had a pair of rubber gloves, called "evening gloves," fastened to the glass wall of the box. Inside the box was a set of tweezers.

Suddenly, a stream of small stones came clattering through the pipe in the ceiling and spilled into the glass sorting box I was watching. A Botswanan sorter immediately went to work. He thrust his hands inside the evening gloves, which protruded into the sealed glass container, and through these gloves, he picked up the tweezers. He quickly separated the stones into two piles - diamonds and non-diamonds. The chief sorter then came over to double-check the sorting. The sorter then pushed the non-diamonds down a hole in one side of the box, where they clanked through a pipe. "Those stones will be fed back onto the conveyor belt just in case the sorter missed any diamonds," Gibson explained.

The diamonds left in the glass box were then released through a trap door in the bottom into a steel container. This container is continually guarded by two Botswana soldiers with shotguns.

The chief sorter allowed me to examine the day's catch of diamonds through a window in the steel container. The vast preponderance of the diamonds was black chips resembling tiny fragments of coal. "What are black diamonds used for?" I asked.

"They're industrial diamonds," Gibson answered. "Most of them are ground down into abrasive grit and used to grind tools and precision parts."

"How much are they worth?" I asked.

"They will probably bring about $2 a carat, which is only a hundredth of what good gem diamonds will fetch in today's market," he replied. He said that it still is financially rewarding since the mine produces about 1.7 million carats of industrial grade diamonds in a year. The mix is roughly 80 percent industrial diamonds and 20 percent gems. The income from the industrial diamonds, even at a mere $2 a carat, is sufficient to pay the day-to-day operating costs of the mine.

I peered again into the box and saw that the whitish diamonds, which looked like tiny pieces of broken glass, had a wide variety of shapes. Some were flat chips, others were twisted triangles, and many were no larger than a grain of sand. It seemed difficult to see how this batch of uncut diamonds could ever be converted into fine jewels.

According to the chief sorter, there were between 1,000 and 1,500 carats of gems in the day's take. He explained that the exact determination of the number of gem stones, and their value, was made by an official appraiser in the Botswana capital of Gaborone. The diamonds were then flown to London.

"How many of those diamonds are large enough to cut into a one-carat engagement stone?" I asked, recalling the concern about dwindling supplies of the large diamonds.

"You might find only two or three of that size here," he said. In light of this low ratio in Botswana, it seemed that the concern was well founded.

When we left the separation plant, I looked at the huge mountain of kimberlite waste behind it. Each day the plant processed and spewed out some 20,000 tons of ore. It seemed to be an incredible undertaking for a mere handful of gem diamonds.

"Gem diamonds can be worth anywhere between $100 and $5,000 a carat depending on their quality," said Gibson, adding, "and quality is, for all practical purposes, what the official appraisers say it is." He explained that appraisers had to take into account such nebulous factors as the shade of color, shape, and the cutability of the uncut diamond in making their evaluation. This evaluation was of considerable importance to the Botswana government, for it derived most of its revenue from the 50 percent share of the profits it received on the diamonds.

Diamond mines, unlike most other kinds of mining operations, could not measure, or even reasonably estimate the value of their own product. Gold mines can calculate how many ounces they produce each day, and copper mines can estimate their tonnage, but the Orapa mine could not immediately determine whether its production of gem diamonds that day was worth $100,000 or a million dollars. Both the diamond mine and the Botswana government had to await the outcome of the official evaluation by the De Beers-trained appraisers.

We had lunch that afternoon at the Orapa Club. During the meal, Gibson told the story of how he and another De Beers geologist named Gavin Lamont discovered the Botswana diamonds.

It began in 1962 when Harry Oppenheimer decided to acquire the prospecting rights in Botswana (which was then the British protectorate of Bechuana land). Prospectors had already discovered three diamonds on the banks of the Moutlouse River, but unable to find the source of the diamonds they had abandoned the search. For nearly four years, Gibson and Lamont scoured the headwaters of the Moutlouse without finding a trace of diamonds - or any of the minerals associated with them. At this point, Lamont came up with a highly speculative geological theory. Since there had been enormous upheavals of the earth's crust in southern Africa in prehistoric times, he suggested that the Moutlouse River may have been truncated by the rising earth; its previous source might have been on the other side of the mountains. Even though there was no corroborative evidence for this theory, Lamont and Gibson believed it was worth the gamble to explore it. They moved their prospecting team north to the edge of the Kalahari Desert.

Sand proved to be an immediate problem for the prospectors. If there was a rich kimberlite pipe in the desert, it would be buried under hundreds of feet of sand and gravel. How could they sample the minerals under the desert?

White ants, which had built towering mounds on the desert, provided the solution. Gibson and Lamont realized that these ants had tunneled hundreds of feet below the surface of the desert in searching for humid earth for their nest, and with the mud they retrieved they also brought up traces of minerals from below the surface. By analyzing samples from these ant colonies, Gibson and Lamont found traces of two other minerals-garnets and ilmenites. Since both these minerals frequently occurred in kimberlite, they had reason to hope they were on the right track.

Finally, in March 1967, Gibson narrowed the search to a spot located a few miles away from a cattle trading camp called "Orapa" by the natives. Here he began drilling for core samples with equipment that De Beers had flown up from its Kimberley headquarters. "Those diamonds literally poured out of the small rotary pan," Gibson recalled. "We realized that we were on to something very big indeed." Gibson next ordered a series of aerial photographs taken of the area. Examining them, he delineated a depression more than a half mile in diameter. It was, in fact, the mouth of the Orapa pipe. "It was quite unbelievable that the whole area could in fact be kimberlite," he remembered thinking then.

From that moment on, De Beers moved quickly to bring the mine into production. It cost some $3.3 million. Four years later, it went into production, and it was officially opened on May 26, 1971, by President Seretse Khania. Oppenheimer, indeed, had the entire Botswana government flown in for the ceremony. "It was, after all, the first diamond mine that De Beers had ever found," Gibson added.

According to Gibson, De Beers had completely missed the 44-acre Finsch pipe in South Africa, and the 360-acre Mwadui pipe in Tanzania, the largest pipe mine ever found, even though both sites had been explored by its geologists several years before the respective discoveries. In every instance, up to the discoveries of Botswana, De Beers simply bought out the others. De Beers presumably had been purposely avoiding unnecessarily expanding the supply of diamonds by uncovering new mines.

December 6, 1978
KINGDOM OF LESOTHO

The twin engine Otter, which De Beers had bought from the US Air Force in Vietnam-and which still carried bullet scars from that war-flew low over the 10,000-foot-high mountains. The kingdom of Lesotho, a landlocked enclave roughly the size of Belgium, was, up until 1966, the British protectorate of Basutoland. Below, I could see the ruins of fortresses used centuries before by the Basutos to defend themselves against the invasions of Zulus and other tribes. The land in the valleys looked green and rich, and trails through the mountain passes led to clusters of huts with conically shaped roofs.

The plane headed directly into a mountain wall shrouded by dense clouds. Everyone aboard, even the South African engineers who made this trip each week, gripped the edge of the seats. There was dead silence in the cabin. The wings of the plane looked as if they were about to touch the rocks they were flying through. Only then did I see the landing strip. It had literally been carved out of the mountainside. The wheels touched with a dull but reassuring thump. The Otter then slowly taxied up a rocky hill, screeched to a stop on the edge of a cliff and in a moment a dozen Basotho workers had tied it down with ropes firmly lashed around its wings and tail.

Through the morning mist, I could discern the rectangular shape of a corrugated iron tower built against the side of the mountain, which, oddly enough, resembled some of the ancient citadels that the plane had passed over. It was, I realized, the separation plant for the diamonds. "Welcome to Letseng-La-Tcrai," the pilot said over the intercom. "It's the highest mine in the world." We were 10,000 feet above sea level on what is called "the roof of Africa." The pilot explained to me, as I sat for a moment recuperating from the landing, that this Otter was the only means of getting in or out of the mine in winter weather.

When I disembarked, I found standing on this mountaintop a tall, slender man impeccably dressed in a three-piece pin-striped suit and wearing a school tie. He seemed completely unruffled and impervious to the icy wind that blew across the mountain. He looked, in fact, as if he had just got out of a cab in the center of London.

"Rogan MacLean," he said, introducing himself. He explained that he worked at the Diamond Trading Company in London, and he had been sent to Lesotho to evaluate the diamonds coming out of its mine. He said that he was in charge of evaluating "large stones," which De Beers defined as any uncut gem diamond weighing over 14.8 carats.

"How many large stones are found every year?" I asked.

"Very few. I'd say well under 200. This mine is one of the few places in the world we regularly get them from," MacLean explained. While we waited for a Land Rover to pick us up, he told me that this mine had only been opened for thirteen months, and it had already produced nearly 100 "large stones." He said that most of these Lesothan diamonds had a brownish tint to them but aside from that they were of first-rate quality. He explained that diamonds can be profitably mined in some of the most inaccessible locations in the world precisely because the operation does not require the construction of a vast transportation infrastructure to remove the final product. Almost all other mining enterprises, such as iron, copper, lead, zinc and potash, need to be built near railroads, pipelines or ports to bulk ship thousands of tons of ore a day. Most precious metals, such as gold, silver and platinum, must be chemically separated from the surrounding matrix of ore in a smelter that in turn usually requires massive daily shipments of coal and other materials. A diamond, however, requires only a primitive landing strip and a light plane to transport its final product which, though it may be worth tens of millions of dollars, seldom amounts to more than a few pounds of stones a day.

"How much are the Lesotho diamonds worth?" I inquired.

McLean estimated that whereas a one-carat diamond in good condition would be sold by the Diamond Trading Company for $300, a two-carat diamond of comparative quality might bring $2,000 and a similar three-carat diamond would fetch $5,400. "When you come to my little specialties, a forty-carat diamond might bring a half million dollars."

Just then a bell began furiously ringing. Something extraordinary had apparently happened at the mine. A moment later, the Land-Rover arrived, and the driver talked with great excitement to MacLean. As we drove off in the Land-Rover, MacLean explained to me that they were ringing a bell because a large diamond had just been found - the first in nearly two weeks.

When we pulled up in front of the sorting house, we were by a youthful man with a craggy face and blue eyes. He introduced himself as Keith Whitelock, the manager of the mine. He seemed visibly elated about this diamond. "Thought we might never find another big stone."

"Now you don't have to worry about closing the mine," MacLean said, with a broad smile. Whitelock winced at this joke. It contained a grain of truth. He told me that he had lived and prospected in Lesotho for over ten years. "Have you ever been to any place this beautiful?" He asked me pointing down the mountain. A stream cut through the emerald green hill below, and then cascaded down over white rocks. Surrounding the hill were snow-covered mountain peaks. "Is it your Shangri-La?" I asked.

"I came here with Colonel Jack Scott twenty years ago and I never left." Scott was a South African adventurer looking for diamonds, and he had heard of a Kimberlite pipe in Lesotho. Even before diamonds had been discovered in South Africa, Basotho tribesmen mined these kimberlites. They had been looking not for diamonds but for a mineral used as a bright cosmetic by the Basotho women. Scott managed to persuade the paramount chieftainess of Lesotho to give him a concession to sift through the ore for diamonds. "We came up on horseback and had to hack a jeep trail up the mountain," Whitelock said, "we were stranded for a week in a blizzard, but we found diamonds."

After Scott gave up the concession, Whitelock continued to prospect on his own in Lesotho. When in 1967, a Basotho woman found a mountain diamond weighing 601 carats, the diamond rush was on. In 1974, Oppenheimer, took over the concession, and hired Whitlock to manage the mine.

Whitelock held up the newly-discovered diamond. "It's a pity it has this crack in it," he said, "otherwise it could have been cut into a marquise shape." He explained that because of this almost invisible crack, the diamond would have to be cut into two separate jewels. "The most you could get out of this is two twelve-carat round diamonds."

MacLean concluded that more than half the weight would be lost in cutting and polishing; depending on the shape of the diamond, somewhere between one-third and one-half of the weight is lost in cutting.

"What about the color?" Whitelock asked.

"The color is superb," MacLean answered, pronouncing "superb" as if it were two distinct words. He pointed out that it was extremely fortunate that the diamond was pure white. If it had a brownish tinge to it, as had the last large diamond he had examined from Lesotho, it would be worth only a tenth as much. "This mine depends on big stones. We need to produce two or three a month just to stay in business," he explained.

When we got to the sorting room, Whitelock instructed the chief sorter to show MacLean the big stone that had just been found. A Basotho guard with a shotgun looked on as the sorter handed the diamond to MacLean.

It was the first large diamond I had seen and it looked like a large piece of broken glass, except that its edges were smooth. MacLean placed it on the scale. It weighed exactly fifty-eight carats. He nodded approvingly and pulled out his jeweler's loupe from his pocket. Looking through it, he examined the diamond for about a minute.

Whitelock perked up and asked MacLean how much money this diamond would fetch in London. This in turn would determine how much money De Beers would credit to the mine's account.

"I'd say it should bring between six and seven thousand dollars a carat," MacLean responded, without hesitating. At minimum, then, this single diamond would be sold to a dealer for $342,000.

"That's enough to keep the mine going for another two weeks," Whitelock said smiling.

He explained that a single stone such as this one, though it weighed a fraction of an ounce, supported a mining enterprise that employed 800 workers for the better part of a month. This was because of low wages. A Basotho worker earned on average only $25 a week. From this amount, De Beers deducts the cost of each worker's food and lodgings. The South African engineers and supervisors, most of who commute to South Africa weekly in the Otter, earned about $250 a week. With other operating expenses, such as fuel for the trucks and electricity for the machinery, the mountaintop mine cost less than $150,000 a week to operate.

Whitelock drove us from the sorting house to the mine itself. Like the desert mine at Orapa, it was a kimberlite pipe. It was, however, only one-thirtieth the size of the pit I had seen the day before in Botswana. "This is the smallest diamond mine that De Beers operates," Whitelock said, as we stood on the edge of the shallow pit. Below, about a dozen Basotho workers were loading a truck with a power shovel. "We also have the dubious distinction of mining the lowest-grade ore of any De Beers mine." He explained that they had to sift through three to four tons of kimberlite at the separation to find a single carat of diamonds. And most of the diamonds found are not of gem quality. In all, this mine had produced only 17,000 carats of gem diamonds in its first year of production.

I recalled that Oppenheimer had told me that De Beers had invested more money in this mountain venture than in any other diamond mine outside of South Africa. It had cost some $45 million to develop even though it produced only a trickle of diamonds.

"There is only one reason for this mine to exist: large stones," Whitelock said.

MacLean added "Movie stars won't want diamonds if you need a magnifying glass to see them." He said one reason why the supply of large stones was diminishing was that most of De Beers' mines fed the kimberlite ore directly into the giant crushers which tended to smash larger diamonds into smaller ones.

The Lesotho mine had a bypass system which could turn up a giant diamond. MacLean said. "You'll save the cost of it with a single diamond some day."

We dined with the supervisory staff in a wood-paneled room that overlooked the spectacular mining site. They had a visitor from the Soviet Union, a geologist named George Smernoff. Smernoff, it turned out, had been stationed in Lesotho for nearly a year to observe De Beers' mining techniques. This arrangement with Smernoff was part of an "exchange" between De Beers and the Soviets.

This remote kingdom seemed an odd place for an "exchange." On the other hand, since the Soviet Union was supposedly boycotting South Africa because of its racial policies, Lesotho provided a convenient official residence for a Soviet mining expert whose unofficial business was in South Africa. "Does Smernoff have access to other De Beers mines?" I asked. No one at the table answered.

December 7, 1978
ORANJEMUND, NAMIBIA

After making a stop in Windhoek, the Anglo-American plane, flew across the Namib Desert to Oranjemund, which is located, as its name implies, at the mouth of the Orange River.

The difference between Oranjemund and the rest of Namibia was that it was not under the control of the South African army. It was, and had been since its inception in 1936, the private preserve of De Beers and its wholly owned subsidiary, Consolidated Diamond Mines.

Oppenheimer's father had built the entire city from scratch after he had obtained exclusive rights to the adjacent 200 miles of Namibian desert called the Sperrgebeit, or "forbidden zone." Cordoned off from the rest of Namibia by two barbwire fences, it has continued to live up to its ominous name. No one, not even army or government officials, is allowed into the forbidden zone without the express permission of Oppenheimer's diamond company.

The forbidden zone was a world unto itself. The only means of entering it was the Ernest Oppenheimer Bridge, which spanned the Orange River frontier between South Africa and Namibia. Armed guards manned two barbwire barricades at both the South African and Namibian ends of the bridge. I was permitted into the forbidden zone only because I had a plastic security badge and an escort, Clive Cowley, the chief public affairs officer of De Beers in Namibia. To enter into the mining area, I inserted my security badge into a slot in the wall and a door then slid open automatically. Cowley explained that the central computer, which opens and closes these passageways, tracks the comings and goings of everyone in the mining area. To prevent any unauthorized intrusions, De Beers's helicopters patrol overhead, and closely monitor the activities of the fishing craft that pass by in the ocean (even though the enormous waves would make landing a boat on the beach all but impossible). Behind the beach, Alsatian guard dogs patrol the no-man's-land between the two barbwire fences. And behind the barbwire fences is the Namib Desert, one of the most inhospitable areas on earth. It is made impenetrable by 1,000-foot-high sand dunes and 120 degree temperatures.

The extraordinary security procedures are considered necessary in Namibia because what is recovered from the 200 mile-long beach is not kimberlite ore but pure gem diamonds, which can be easily pocketed by anyone. In one small crevice in a rock outcropping, Cowley, a chatty former newspaperman, told me a guard found 15,000 carats of sparkling diamonds on this beach some years ago.

The "mine," if it can be called a mine, is actually the continental shelf of the Atlantic Ocean. To get at the richest lodes of diamonds, the ocean must be literally pushed back and held back long enough to dig out the diamonds. The mechanism for holding back the pounding surf is a ten-story high mound, which, 600 feet out in the ocean, runs parallel to the beach.

Standing on this sandy mound, I looked down into the "mine," which was actually the exposed floor of the ocean. It was an incredible sight; a full-scale battle between man and nature.

"You are looking at the largest construction project in the Southern Hemisphere," observed Cowley. He pointed to the thousands of workers and machines below. Giant bulldozers were belching smoke and scraping the ground with their blades like some kind of prehistoric animal. Powerful pumps were sucking the water out of the mining area through hoses as fast as it sprayed in over the barrier. Ovambo tribesmen, knee-deep in pools of water, were frantically sweeping the gravel off outcrops of rock on the ocean's floor as if they feared that at any moment the barrier might give way, like a sand castle on a beach, and the ocean would come flooding in.

In the center of all this activity was an enormous piece of machinery, more than a football field in length and two stories high, mounted on caterpillar tracks. A continuous belt of steel buckets traveled around it, like cars on a Ferris wheel, scooping up sand at one end and depositing it at the other end. It was the largest machine I had ever seen.

"That's the bucket wheel excavator," Cowley explained. "It cost $3.5 million to build, and it can move 1,800 tons of sand an hour." The sand must be stripped away before the workers, called lashers, can get at the diamond-rich gravel.

The Ovambo tribesmen worked with their primitive tools in the shadow of this colossal machine. The contrast between tribal and modern technology was striking. Ironically, as Cowley pointed out, it was the tribesmen, not the multi-million-dollar machine, who recovered most of the diamonds. These Ovambos had been recruited to work in the ocean mine in the jungles of Ovamba land, a thousand miles to the north. According to Cowley, they usually received eight-month contracts from the diamond company. They would board a Hercules cargo plane, leaving their families behind on the kraal, and fly to Oranjemund.

"They have to be literally fought off the plane," Cowley said. For just sweeping the gravel from the rocks, they received $200 a month. For driving trucks and other more skilled jobs, they earned up to $450 a month. This salary is completely exempt from taxes. Their own expense for their eight-month stay at the mines is $22 a month for their dormitory room and food. "By the time they return to Ovamba land, they have enough money to buy cattle, land or even a wife," Cowley concluded.

Suddenly, a tractor the size of a locomotive raced toward us. As it passed, an Ovambo waved from the cab. He then maneuvered the vehicle precariously on the edge of the mound, which was only about sixty feet wide, and dumped a load of dirt on top of it. Cowley explained that these tractors wage an around-the-clock battle with the Atlantic Ocean. Waves constantly rip away the sand, and these tractors, each of which carries a thirty-five-ton load of sand, constantly fill the breeches in the barrier. If an opening were not immediately filled, the ocean would break through and submerge the entire mine under fifty feet of sea water.

Every day, more than 100 million pounds of sand and gravel are dug out of the ocean mine. From the massive moving of the earth and holding back of the ocean, about two and a half to three pounds of diamonds are recovered each day. "All this effort, and more, purely for the vanity of women," Cowley added, with an edge of irony in his voice. That irony was only compounded by the fact that De Beers had millions of dollars invested in advertising to take advantage of this vanity.

When I viewed the day's catch in the sorting house, which was that day about 6,000 carats, I saw that unlike in Botswana and Lesotho there were no black or discolored diamonds in the tray. These were clearly not industrial-grade diamonds, but white, well-formed gem diamonds.

"These aren't the same sort of diamonds that come out of a pipe mine," Cowley said. "They have been pounded by ocean waves for millions of years. The inferior diamonds have been smashed to bits eons ago. Only the fittest survive, and these are pure gems."

Pointing to the container of diamonds that had been recovered from the ocean floor that day, he continued, "There are probably more pure gems in that dish than have been recovered today in all the pipe mines in South Africa combined." Cowley estimated that this single day's production would bring in over $1-5 million when they were sold by De Beers in London.

The profits on these Namibian diamonds were enormous. It cost no more to mine and separate these gem diamonds than it did for the industrial-grade diamonds that constituted the bulk of the production of most other mines. Yet these gems sold for one hundred times the price of industrial diamonds. From the four-hundred million dollars in revenues it took in the preceding year for these Namibian diamonds, De Beers realized a net profit of more than two hundred million dollars, making Namibia De Beers' money spinner.

After we left the sorting house, Cowley took me over to see an extraordinary scrap yard. It was enclosed by barbwire; and filled with enough antique machines to stock a museum. "Once a vehicle or piece of equipment ever enters the mining area, it is never allowed to leave," Cowley said. He explained that this prohibition was necessary in order to prevent anyone from smuggling diamonds out concealed in a piece of equipment. Since it was not practical to attempt to search for an object as small as a diamond, De Beers simply assigned all the vehicles and machines, when they became outmoded, to this graveyard.

This tangle of relics encapsulated the history of the Namibian diamonds. There was, for example, a train of turn-of-the-century railroad cars with German markings. "Namibia was a German colony when diamonds were first found here at the turn of the century," Cowley said. He explained that the diamond fields were then about 100 miles north of Oranjemund. To mine the diamonds, the Germans had built Teutonic towns at Pomona and Kolinanskop, complete with beer halls and skittle alleys. "The Germans had the blacks sweep the streets every day to keep the sand out of their houses. When they could no longer find any diamonds on the beaches they abandoned these towns to the desert. It has become a ghost town; the beer hall is now filled with sand, which comes halfway to the walls inside the houses."

There was also an ominous-looking World War II battle tank with a British insignia on it. A huge steel blade had been welded in front of the gun turret. "De Beers converted these tanks to bulldozers after the war," Cowley continued, "because there was no bridge across the Orange River then and it was next to impossible to float heavy equipment across on barges." It took until the mid nineteen-fifties before the bridge was built.

Since De Beers' geologist found that most of the diamond lodes were on the ocean floor, a method had to be devised of holding the ocean back, Cowley explained. Assisted by oceanographers at the University of Capetown, engineers initially experimented with the idea of altering the ocean's current so that it would rip up the beach and redeposit the sand farther from the shoreline. This would create a natural barrier behind which the workers could sweep the diamonds out from the bedrock. To shift the direction of the ocean current, they dug a channel across the beach. Unfortunately, the ocean refused to follow the predicted course, and the engineers gave up on the attempt to harness the sea.

Next, the engineers attempted to erect an earthen dam in the ocean at low tide and cover it with a gigantic canvas tarpaulin before the tide returned. They postulated that the tarpaulin would prevent the ocean from dissolving the dam. Working in a rising tide, it took nearly two hours to lash down this cover. Less than an hour later, the waves ripped the tarpaulin to shreds.

The De Beers engineers had to return to their drawing boards. Finally, in the early 1960s, they came up with a system for building a series of dams that would be replenished with sand from the mine as fast as the ocean could strip it away. "After a good deal of trial and error it worked," Cowley concluded.

Leaving the mining area, we had to pass through a long narrow building. Along one wall were large mirrors, which, Cowley explained, were two-way glasses through which security guards observed everyone passing through. At the end of one maze-like corridor, there was a turnstile that led to two closed doors, side by side. We went through the turnstile, waited; then a buzzer sounded, and the door on the right opened. "If the other door had opened, you would have had to undergo both an X-ray and body search," Cowley said. He explained that the selection of who gets searched is completely at random. It would be medically dangerous to subject workers to constant dosages of X-rays, therefore only a small percentage of those who passed out of the mining area each day were actually searched. "Everyone from Harry Oppenheimer to Ovambo workers has to pass through that turnstile, and they never know which door is going to open," Cowley added, as he again inserted our security badges into the slot at the end of the passageway.

The last door buzzed opened, and a moment later we were walking down a suburban street in Oranjemund. The transition from the moonscape-like mine to the familiarity of the modern city was somewhat unsettling.

I dined that evening at the Hexen Kessel, a restaurant whose decor and cuisine were meant to evoke an "Old World" European spirit in the middle of the Namib Desert. At dinner, I met Richard Wake-Walker, a young executive at the Diamond Trading Corporation, who had flown in from London to take stock, as he put it, "of the catch of ocean diamonds." He proved to be a keen observer of the incongruity of the entire Namibian diamond mining venture. Outside of this enclave, the SWAPO guerrillas with their primitive arms were waging a bitter war against South Africa's control of Namibia. Inside it, among the ghost towns in the sand, De Beers was using its state-of-the art machines to harvest a bonanza of diamonds from the ocean.

"What if SWAPO wins and forces De Beers to relinquish its concession? I asked.

"Not much of a problem," he answered. "De Beers would withdraw, the ocean would flood back into the fields, and the diamonds would be unrecoverable."

"Wouldn't the loss of the diamonds be a problem?" I asked, confused by his answer."

"Don't be naive," he answered with a good-natured smile. "The success of De Beers of De Beers does not depend on producing more diamonds -- the world has enough -- it depends on controlling how many get put on the market."

December 14, 1978
KIMBERLEY, SOUTH AFRICA

In 1978, there were only six underground diamond mines in the world. Five of them were here in the mining city of Kimberley (and the sixth was 400 miles northeast in the Transvaal.) The Wesselton, located only about a mile from downtown Kimberley, was the deepest of these diamond mines. The mine shaft extended 3,300 feet below the surface.

Before I was allowed to descend into the Wesselton, I was taken to a spotlessly clean changing room and provided with the necessary mining gear. This included steel boots, a white jumpsuit, a steel helmet with a built-in lantern, and a portable battery, which I strapped around my waist. I then proceeded to the mine shaft where I was met by Edward Robinson, a soft-spoken South African, who had been born and raised in the mining area around Kimberley.

At the top of the mine shaft, we stepped into a steel cage, the size of a large freight elevator. The door clanged shut. Robinson pressed a button, and with a sudden jerk, we began hurtling down the mine shaft. We were falling at a rate of twenty feet per second, or twelve miles an hour. Even at that speed, it took slightly more than two minutes to reach the mining level, 2,500 feet below the surface.

From all the films I had seen about coal mining, I expected to step out into a dark tunnel where men were hacking away at the rock with picks and shovels. Instead, I found myself standing in an enormous well-lightand air-conditioned chamber. The ceiling was at least fifteen feet high, and there was a road in it wide enough for a two-ton truck.

"We call this the block cavina method," Robinson said. "It works on the same principle as punching a hole in the bottom of a bottle to drain the liquid out." He explained that rather than scooping out the kimberlite ore from above, as is done in open-pit mining, a shaft is drilled in the bedrock that encases the volcanic pipe. Once underneath the main body of ore in the pipe, or "the bottom of the bottle," as Robinson put it, a series of tunnels that run parallel to the surface are dug under the pipe. This is the "mining level." The kimberlite above, loosened by dynamite, and then simply pours into the tunnels.

Robinson's attention focused on something happening at the end of the tunnel we were entering. He held up his hand. Suddenly, everyone around us froze.

A voice counted in Afrikaner "... schwi ... di ... ein." Then there was a loud explosion, followed in rapid succession by four other blasts. I could feel the reverberations of the concussion and smell burnt sulphur in the air.

"They're dynamiting ahead," Robinson calmly said. The dynamite came, he explained, from De Beers' own explosive factory, which was the largest in Africa.

Robinson motioned to follow him into the tunnel. At one end, kimberlite ore was flooding in. A black worker operated a powerful winch. It manipulated a bulldozer blade about thirty yards away. The blade scraped kimberlite ore through a hole in the floor of the tunnel.

The ore poured into a train of hopper cars on the level below. It was fully automated. The train arrives under the opening just before the scraper forces the ore through it. When full, it then shuttles over to the mine shaft where it dumps its ore. A belt of continuous buckets then bring the ore to the surface and deposits it on the conveyor belt. In all, this highly mechanized form of mining required about 165 men, including supervisors, below ground. Most of the workers were black, and the supervisors were white.

Robinson said that it was the white labor unions who insisted that the whites be given supervisory positions, rather than the blacks. He explained that some 40 percent of the black workers were tribesmen from Lesotho on seasonal contracts (while in South Africa, they lived in De Beers-owned dormitories, called "hostels," and received about $40 a week in salary).

Before Robinson became manager of the Wesselton mine he had worked at one of the Anglo-owned gold mines. The mining level there was more than one mile below the surface of the earth, and the temperature of the walls in the cramped tunnels reached 120 degrees Fahrenheit. Unlike kimberlite, which when loosened flows by gravity into the mining tunnels, gold ore must be chiseled out of bedrock with picks and drills. "The seam at times was no wider than a pencil line, and there were literally thousands of men chipping away at it," he said. "There are more workers in a single gold mine than in all the De Beers diamond mines in South Africa."

When we returned to the surface, I was momentarily blinded by the glare of the sun. It was also at least thirty degrees warmer above ground than below. We then took another elevator to the top of the tower of the mine shaft, which were about ten stories high. From this vantage point, the entire history of the mine could be clearly seen.

Robinson pointed to a yawning pit, almost 500 feet deep, across the parched earth. It was the original mine. Like all pipe mines, the Wesselton had begun as an open-pit mine. At some point it became too deep to haul out the kimberlite ore profitably. "The only way it could be mined," Robinson said, was "to get the ore out from below."

The half-mile-deep mine I had just visited was below that pit. The continuous belt of buckets dumped the ore from the shaft onto the conveyor belt. At Wesselton, according to Robinson, more than 6,000 tons of kimberlite ore is brought up the mine shaft every day by this automated equipment. Yet there are only some 1,400 carats of diamonds recovered from this mass of ore. Of these, only about 150 carats are of gem quality. "More diamonds are recovered per ton from the waste dumps than from the mines", he said, pointing to the mountains of kimberlite ore that had been spewed out of the separation plants over the years.

Some of this waste was more than a hundred years old. Diamonds smaller than a tenth of a carat were difficult to sell then, and De Beers had not invested until recently in sophisticated technology for recovering a high proportion of the minute diamonds. Now, however, with factories in India polishing diamonds as small as 1/25th of a carat, there was a ready market for these "small goods."

Even with the "mining" of the old dumps, Robinson admitted that the Wesselton and the other mines around Kimberley were rapidly reaching the point of diminishing returns. He estimated that the De Beers mines in Kimberley could begin to run out of gem diamonds as early as the 1980s. Kimberley might then become a ghost town.

It was here that the diamond invention was devised, and the inseparable connection between Kimberley and De Beers, which is still evident when one, walks through the town. The zigzagging streets follow the pattern of the original mining claims. They then end abruptly in an enormous crater that the city literally hangs over. It is about one-quarter of a mile deep and partly filled with rain water, which reflects the buildings on the edge of the city. This abyss is called the Big Hole, and it is what remains of the Kimberley Central mine. This was the deepest open-pit mine ever dug. The ore was lifted out by a system of ropes and pulleys that looked like a giant spider web. Before it was finally abandoned in 1914, it produced over three and a half tons of diamonds. This flood of diamonds not only transformed Kimberley into a city, but it necessitated the creation of a global system for distributing and controlling the sale of diamonds.

After I ascended from the mine, I got dressed and went to the Kimberley Club for lunch. I was sat next to Barry Hawthorne, a De Beers geologist who had recently returned from Siberia in the Soviet Union, I asked him if the Siberian mines were similar to the ones in Kimberley.

"It is very odd; the mines in South Africa produce few diamonds over time. The mine in Siberia seems to produce more diamonds every year. It is an enigma."

December 15, 1978
KIMBERLEY, SOUTH AFRICA

I went at 9 am to the Harry Oppenheimer House, a darkly tinted glass skyscraper that stands in a private park in the center of Kimberley. It is the portal through which the diamonds are exported. Built in 1974, the entire building was designed and dedicated to a single purpose: the evaluation of uncut diamonds. The entire total of all the diamond mines and diggings in South Africa and Namibia are shipped here to be sorted, classified and valued. The diamond consignments generally arrive early in the morning in armored trucks, which drive into a concrete bunker in the sub basement of the building. The sealed containers of diamonds are then sent in a special elevator, which makes no intermediary stops, to the top floor. The seal is broken in front of witnesses, and the diamonds immersed in an acid bath to clean off any particles of dirt. After the diamonds are dried by hot-air jets, they are weighed on a highly precise electronic scale. This weight is then entered into a central computer, which will track the shipment as it moves through each stage in the sorting process.

If at any point the weight of the categories it has been divided into adds up to less than the original weight of the consignment, the computer sets off an alarm. This automatically locks the doors of the Harry Oppenheimer House. Only when the missing weight of diamonds is found will the computer permit anyone to leave the building.

Unlike gold or other precious metals, diamonds cannot be assigned a value merely by weighing them. An ounce of diamonds can be worth $100 or $100,000 depending on the quality of the diamonds. Before either a mine - or the South African tax authorities - can determine the value of the diamonds, they have to be sorted into their proper size, shape, color and clarity categories. "By the time we finish, a shipment is broken down into some two thousand different categories. The preliminary sorting is done by a series of ingenious machines that De Beers' engineers invented specifically for this purpose. First, the diamonds are passed through a series of sieves. Diamonds that are too small to be cut into jewels are screened out as industrial diamonds. The remaining diamonds are then divided into sixteen different groups according to sizes that range from under two-tenths of a carat to over one carat.

Next, within each group, the diamonds are sorted for shape by a series of machines, which by vibrating and twisting are able to separate flat and triangular shapes from the more valuable tetrahedral-shaped diamonds. At each stage in the separation process, the resulting groups are weighed and registered into the computer.

Finally, in this rough sorting, the diamonds are fed into a series of

X-ray machines, which by employing different filters are able to automatically sort the diamonds into different colors. The opaque and black diamonds, called boart, as well as the smaller brown and golden diamonds, are separated out to be crushed into industrial abrasives. The diamonds are then again reweighed and sent to the floor below for hand sorting.

Here the gem-grade diamonds are laid out by colors on separate tables, which have been perfectly positioned in respect to the light. A team of sorters, women in uniformly colored dresses and men in suits, then examine each diamond with a six-power jewelers' loupe to make sure that it is correctly classified. If any of the five sorters disagrees in their opinion, the chief sorter, John Gie, is called in to arbitrate and make a final decision on that particular diamond.

"These are all highly skilled and trained quality controllers," Gie explained to me. All are given periodic eye examinations by De Beers and are tested on their ability to match unsorted diamonds to the De Beers sample set. This set contains some 240 different shades of colors and shapes which serve as a De Beers standard for sorting operations in both Kimberley and London. After every gem diamond is checked for microscopic imperfections representatives of the Diamond Producers Association, which represents individual producers as well as the De Beers-owned mines, are allowed to question any classification they disagree with. In fact this generally is nothing more than a formality.

"A single diamond can be examined as many as ten times," observed Gie. When everyone has agreed on the proper classification of each diamond, the data is fed into the computer. As each diamond is finally weighed, the computer assigns a dollar value to it according to a complex formula. The computer then instantly tallies up the total value of the shipment and credits that amount to the account of the individual mine.

A small percentage of these sorted diamonds are retained at Harry Oppenheimer House and distributed to a select number of local South African dealers. All the rest of the diamonds of South Africa and Namibia are shipped in sealed containers by air to the Diamond Trading Company's headquarters in London. These consignments from Kimberley amounted to some 5,400,000 carats and accounted for about half of the entire gem diamonds shipped to the Diamond

Trading Company in London.

This "single channel," as Gie termed it, was at the heart of De Beers' control of the market. It allowed it to restrict the number of diamonds that ever reached diamond cutters, and, ultimately, the public.

December 17, 1978
JOHANNESBURG, SOUTH AFRICA

Albert Jolis had been recommended to me by James Jesus Angleton, the former CIA counterintelligence chief, who had known him as a top intelligence officer in the OSS in World War II. When I told Angleton I was going to Africa to investigate the De Beers cartel, he said, "If anyone can tell you the inside story, it is Bert Jolis."

As it turned out, Jolis was in Johannesburg. We met at the Club 50 at the top of the tallest building in Africa, the 50-story high Carlton Center in downtown Johannesburg. Jolis, though in his early sixties, was a powerhouse of energy. He had arrived the previous day from the Central Africa Empire, where he had negotiated a diamond concession with Emperor Bokassa for his company Diamond Distributors, Inc, en route to London. His family had a long history in the diamond trade. His grandfather, Abraham Jolis, was a diamond cutter in Amsterdam. His father, Jac Jolis, was a director of De Beers in the 1920s and then in the 1930s established a diamond-cutting factory in Los Angeles called the Diamond Development Corporation and pioneered the art of product placement for De Beers by giving diamonds to Hollywood producers who put scenes in movies that linked diamonds to romance. It was the only De Beers-backed venture in the United States. Then De Beers became concerned that the US operation could expose it to a looming anti-trust suit, and abruptly cut off its supply of its diamonds. The factory was closed and Albert Jolis sought his own supply of diamonds by negotiating concessions with African nations outside the purview of De Beers.

Jolis proved to be very perceptive. After I told him about my tour of the diamond mines, he asked "Did Harry Oppenheimer also invite you to a safari at his private Game Park?"

"I am planning to go next week," I answered.

"They will drive you around for an hour in a Landrover and lions, zebras, and rhinos will pop out of the bush. I guarantee it."

"How can you guarantee wild animals in the jungle?"

"It's easy. When they take VIPs out on a safari, they truck out the animals to strategic points, and release them."
"It's stage managed?" I asked.

"It is what De Beers does best, managing illusions." Jolis added, "Oppenheimer arranged for you to see his state-of-the-art mines in Africa, but not the only mine whose output really matters to the cartel."

"Where is that?" I asked.

"London." He answered, without missing a beat. "The De Beers stockpile in its London vault contains all the diamonds it has kept from depressing the market over the past half-century. It is the richest mine in the world, tens of millions of carats, stockpiled in every size, shape, and quality."

"What would happen if De Beers released them on the market?"

"Diamond prices would crash," he said, pointing towards the floor. "It would be the end of one of the most brilliant illusion ever devised."

***

I

HAVE YOU EVER TRIED TO SELL A DIAMOND?

The diamond invention -- the creation of the idea that diamonds are rare and valuable, and are essential signs of esteem -- is a relatively recent development in the history of the diamond trade. Until the late nineteenth century, diamonds were found only in a few riverbeds in India and in the jungles of Brazil, and the entire world production of gem diamonds amounted to a few pounds a year. In 1870, however, huge diamond mines were discovered near the Orange River, in South Africa, where diamonds were soon being scooped out by the ton. Suddenly, the market was deluged with diamonds. The British financiers who had organized the South African mines quickly realized that their investment was endangered; diamonds had little intrinsic value -- and their price depended almost entirely on their scarcity. The financiers feared that when new mines were developed in South Africa, diamonds would become at best only semiprecious gems.

The major investors in the diamond mines realized that they had no alternative but to merge their interests into a single entity that would be powerful enough to control production and perpetuate the illusion of scarcity of diamonds. The instrument they created, in 1888, was called De Beers Consolidated Mines, Ltd., incorporated in South Africa. As De Beers took control of all aspects of the world diamond trade, it assumed many forms. In London, it operated under the innocuous name of the Diamond Trading Company. In Israel, it was known as "The Syndicate." In Europe, it was called the "C.S.O." -- initials referring to the Central Selling Organization, which was an arm of the Diamond Trading Company. And in black Africa, it disguised its South African origins under subsidiaries with names like Diamond Development Corporation and Mining Services, Inc. At its height -- for most of this century -- it not only either directly owned or controlled all the diamond mines in southern Africa but also owned diamond trading companies in England, Portugal, Israel, Belgium, Holland, and Switzerland.

De Beers proved to be the most successful cartel arrangement in the annals of modern commerce. While other commodities, such as gold, silver, copper, rubber, and grains, fluctuated wildly in response to economic conditions, diamonds have continued, with few exceptions, to advance upward in price every year since the Depression. Indeed, the cartel seemed so superbly in control of prices -- and unassailable -- that, in the late 1970s, even speculators began buying diamonds as a guard against the vagaries of inflation and recession.

THE DIAMOND INVENTION

The diamond invention is far more than a monopoly for fixing diamond prices; it is a mechanism for converting tiny crystals of carbon into universally recognized tokens of wealth, power, and romance. To achieve this goal, De Beers had to control demand as well as supply. Both women and men had to be made to perceive diamonds not as marketable precious stones but as an inseparable part of courtship and married life. To stabilize the market, De Beers had to endow these stones with a sentiment that would inhibit the public from ever reselling them. The illusion had to be created that diamonds were forever -- "forever" in the sense that they should never be resold.

In September of 1938, Harry Oppenheimer, son of the founder of De Beers and then twenty-nine, traveled from Johannesburg to New York City, to meet with Gerald M. Lauck, the president of N. W. Ayer, a leading advertising agency in the United States. Lauck and N. W. Ayer had been recommended to Oppenheimer by the Morgan Bank, which had helped his father consolidate the De Beers financial empire. His bankers were concerned about the price of diamonds, which had declined worldwide.

In Europe, where diamond prices had collapsed during the Depression, there seemed little possibility of restoring public confidence in diamonds. In Germany, Austria, Italy, and Spain, the notion of giving a diamond ring to commemorate an engagement had never taken hold. In England and France, diamonds were still presumed to be jewels for aristocrats rather than the masses. Furthermore, Europe was on the verge of war, and there seemed little possibility of expanding diamond sales. This left the United States as the only real market for De Beers's diamonds. In fact, in 1938 some three quarters of the entire cartel's diamonds were sold for engagement rings in the United States. Most of these stones, however, were smaller and of poorer quality than those bought in Europe, and had an average price of $80 apiece. Oppenheimer and the bankers believed that an advertising campaign could persuade Americans to buy more expensive diamonds.

Oppenheimer suggested to Lauck that his agency prepare a plan for creating a new image for diamonds among Americans. He assured Lauck that De Beers had not called on any other American advertising agency with this proposal, and that if the plan met with his father's approval, N. W. Ayer would be the exclusive agents for the placement of newspaper and radio advertisements in the US. Oppenheimer agreed to underwrite the costs of the research necessary for developing the campaign. Lauck instantly accepted the offer.

In their subsequent investigation of the American diamond market, the staff of N. W. Ayer found that since the end of World War I, in 1919, the total amount of diamonds sold in America, measured in carats, had declined by 50 percent; at the same time, the quality of the diamonds, measured in dollar value, had declined by nearly 100 percent. An Ayer memo concluded that the depressed state of the market for diamonds was "the result of the economy, changes in social attitudes and the promotion of competitive luxuries."

Although it could do little about the state of the economy, N. W. Ayer suggested that through a well-orchestrated advertising and public-relations campaign it could have a significant impact on the "social attitudes of the public at large and thereby channel American spending toward larger and more expensive diamonds instead of "competitive luxuries." Specifically, the Ayer study stressed the need to strengthen the association in the public's mind of diamonds with romance. Since "young men buy over 90% of all engagement rings" it would be crucial to inculcate in them the idea that diamonds were a gift of love: the larger and finer the diamond, the greater the expression of love. Similarly, young women had to be encouraged to view diamonds as an integral part of any romantic courtship.

Since the Ayer plan to romanticize diamonds required subtly altering the public's picture of the way a man courts -- and wins -- a woman, the advertising agency strongly suggested exploiting the relatively new medium of motion pictures. Movie idols, the paragons of romance for the mass audience, would be given diamonds to use as their symbols of indestructible love. In addition, the agency suggested offering stories and society photographs to selected magazines and newspapers which would reinforce the link between diamonds and romance. Stories would stress the size of diamonds that celebrities presented to their loved ones, and photographs would conspicuously show the glittering stone on the hand of a well-known woman. Fashion designers would talk on radio programs about the "trend towards diamonds" that Ayer planned to start. The Ayer plan also envisioned using the British royal family to help foster the romantic allure of diamonds. An Ayer memo said, "Since Great Britain has such an important interest in the diamond industry, the royal couple could be of tremendous assistance to this British industry by wearing diamonds rather than other jewels." Queen Elizabeth later went on a well-publicized trip to several South African diamond mines, and she accepted a diamond from Oppenheimer.

In addition to putting these plans into action, N. W. Ayer placed a series of lush four-color advertisements in magazines that were presumed to mold elite opinion, featuring reproductions of famous paintings by such artists as Picasso, Derain, Dali, and Dufy. The advertisements were intended to convey the idea that diamonds, like paintings, were unique works of art.

By 1941, the advertising agency reported to its client that it had already achieved impressive results in its campaign. The sale of diamonds had increased by 55 percent in the United States since 1938, reversing the previous downward trend in retail sales. N. W. Ayer noted also that its campaign had required "the conception of a new form of advertising which has been widely imitated ever since. There was no direct sale to be made. There was no brand name to be impressed on the public mind. There was simply an idea -- the eternal emotional value surrounding the diamond." It further claimed that "a new type of art was devised... and a new color, diamond blue, was created and used in these campaigns..."

In its 1947 strategy plan, the advertising agency strongly emphasized a psychological approach. "We are dealing with a problem in mass psychology. We seek to... strengthen the tradition of the diamond engagement ring -- to make it a psychological necessity capable of competing successfully at the retail level with utility goods and services..." It defined as its target audience "some 70 million people 15 years and over whose opinion we hope to influence in support of our objectives." N. W. Ayer outlined a subtle program that included arranging for lecturers to visit high schools across the country. "All of these lectures revolve around the diamond engagement ring, and are reaching thousands of girls in their assemblies, classes and informal meetings in our leading educational institutions," the agency explained in a memorandum to De Beers. The agency had organized, in 1946, a weekly service called "Hollywood Personalities," which provided 125 leading newspapers with descriptions of the diamonds worn by movie stars. And it continued its efforts to encourage news coverage of celebrities displaying diamond rings as symbols of romantic involvement. In 1947, the agency commissioned a series of portraits of "engaged socialites." The idea was to create prestigious "role models" for the poorer middle-class wage-earners. The advertising agency explained, in its 1948 strategy paper, "We spread the word of diamonds worn by stars of screen and stage, by wives and daughters of political leaders, by any woman who can make the grocer's wife and the mechanic's sweetheart say "I wish I had what she has."

De Beers needed a slogan for diamonds that expressed both the theme of romance and legitimacy. An N. W. Ayer copywriter came up with the caption "A Diamond Is Forever," which was scrawled on the bottom of a picture of two young lovers on a honeymoon. Even though diamonds can in fact be shattered, chipped, discolored, or incinerated to ash, the concept of eternity perfectly captured the magical qualities that the advertising agency wanted to attribute to diamonds. Within a year, "A Diamond Is Forever" became the official motto of De Beers.

In 1951, N. W. Ayer found some resistance to its million-dollar publicity blitz. It noted in its annual strategy review:

"The millions of brides and brides-to-be are subjected to at least two important pressures that work against the diamond engagement ring. Among the more prosperous, there is the sophisticated urge to be different as a means of being smart.... the lower-income groups would like to show more for the money than they can find in the diamond they can afford."

To remedy these problems, the advertising agency argued, "It is essential that these pressures be met by the constant publicity to show that only the diamond is everywhere accepted and recognized as the symbol of betrothal."

N. W. Ayer was always searching for new ways to influence American public opinion. Not only did it organize a service to "release to the women's pages the engagement ring" but it set about exploiting the relatively new medium of television by arranging for actresses and other celebrities to wear diamonds when they appeared before the camera. It also established a "Diamond Information Center" that placed a stamp of quasi-authority on the flood of "historical" data and "news" it released. "We work hard to keep ourselves known throughout the publishing world as the source of information on diamonds," N. W. Ayer commented in a memorandum to De Beers, and added: "Because we have done it successfully, we have opportunities to help with articles originated by others."N. W. Ayer proposed to apply to the diamond market Thorstein Veblen's idea, stated in The Theory of the Leisure Class, that Americans were motivated in their purchases not by utility but by "conspicuous consumption." "The substantial diamond gift can be made a more widely sought symbol of personal and family success -- an expression of socio-economic achievement," N. W. Ayer said in a report. To exploit this desire for conspicuous display, the agency specifically recommended, "Promote the diamond as one material object which can reflect, in a very personal way, a man's... success in life." Since this campaign would be addressed to upwardly mobile men, the advertisements ideally "should have the aroma of tweed, old leather and polished wood which is characteristic of a good club."

Toward the end of the 1950s, N. W. Ayer reported to De Beers that twenty years of advertisements and publicity had a pronounced effect on the American psyche. "Since 1939 an entirely new generation of young people has grown to marriageable age," it said. "To this new generation a diamond ring is considered a necessity to engagements by virtually everyone." The message had been so successfully impressed on the minds of this generation that those who could not afford to buy a diamond at the time of their marriage would "defer the purchase" rather than forgo it.

The campaign to internationalize the diamond invention began in earnest in the mid-1960s. The prime targets were Japan, Germany, and Brazil. Since N. W. Ayer was primarily an American advertising agency, De Beers brought in the J. Walter Thompson agency, which had especially strong advertising subsidiaries in the target countries, to place most of its international advertising. Within ten years, De Beers succeeded beyond even its most optimistic expectations, creating a billion-dollar-a-year diamond market in Japan, where matrimonial custom had survived feudal revolutions, world wars, industrialization, and even the American occupation.

Until the mid-1960s, Japanese parents arranged marriages for their children through trusted intermediaries. The ceremony was consummated, according to Shinto law, by the bride and groom drinking rice wine from the same wooden bowl. There was no tradition of romance, courtship, seduction, or prenuptial love in Japan; and none that required the gift of a diamond engagement ring. Even the fact that millions of American soldiers had been assigned to military duty in Japan for a decade had not created any substantial Japanese interest in giving diamonds as a token of love.

J. Walter Thompson began its campaign by suggesting that diamonds were a visible sign of modern Western values. It created a series of color advertisements in Japanese magazines showing beautiful women displaying their diamond rings. All the women had Western facial features and wore European clothes. Moreover, the women in most of the advertisements were involved in some activity -- such as bicycling, camping, yachting, ocean swimming, or mountain climbing -- that defied Japanese traditions. In the background, there usually stood a Japanese man, also attired in fashionable European clothes. In addition, almost all of the automobiles, sporting equipment, and other artifacts in the picture were conspicuous foreign imports. The message was clear: diamonds represent a sharp break with the Oriental past and a sign of entry into modern life.

The campaign was remarkably successful. Until 1959, the importation of diamonds had not even been permitted by the postwar Japanese government. When the campaign began, in 1967, not quite 5 percent of engaged Japanese women received a diamond engagement ring. By 1972, the proportion had risen to 27 percent. By 1978, half of all Japanese women who were married wore a diamond; by 1981, some 60 percent of Japanese brides wore diamonds. In a mere fourteen years, the 1,500-year Japanese tradition had been radically revised. Diamonds became a staple of the Japanese marriage. Japan became the second largest market, after the United States, for the sale of diamond engagement rings.

In America, which remained the most important market for most of De Beer's diamonds, N. W. Ayer recognized the need to create a new demand for diamonds among long-married couples. "Candies come, flowers come, furs come," but such ephemeral gifts fail to satisfy a woman's psychological craving for "a renewal of the romance," N. W. Ayer said in a report. An advertising campaign could instill the idea that the gift of a second diamond, in the later years of marriage, would be accepted as a sign of "ever-growing love." In 1962, N. W. Ayer asked for authorization to "begin the long-term process of setting the diamond aside as the only appropriate gift for those later-in-life occasions where sentiment is to be expressed." De Beers immediately approved the campaign.

THE RUSSIAN EMBRACE

The diamond market had to be further restructured in the mid-1960s to accommodate a surfeit of minute diamonds, which De Beers undertook to market for the Soviets. They had discovered diamond mines in Siberia, after intensive exploration, in the late 1950s: De Beers and its allies no longer controlled the diamond supply, and realized that open competition with the Soviets would inevitably lead, as Harry Oppenheimer gingerly put it, to "price fluctuations," which would weaken the carefully cultivated confidence of the public in the value of diamonds. Oppenheimer, assuming that neither party could afford risking the destruction of the diamond invention, offered the Soviets a straightforward deal -- "a single channel" for controlling the world supply of diamonds. In accepting this arrangement, the Soviets became partners in the cartel, and co-protectors of the diamond invention.

Almost all of the Soviet diamonds were less than half a carat in their uncut form, and there was no ready retail outlet for millions of such tiny diamonds. When it made its secret deal with the Soviet Union, De Beers had expected production from the Siberian mines to decrease gradually. Instead, production accelerated at an incredible pace, and De Beers was forced to reconsider its sales strategy. De Beers ordered N. W. Ayer to reverse one of its themes: women were no longer to be led to equate the status and emotional commitment to an engagement with the sheer size of the diamond. A "strategy for small diamond sales" was outlined, stressing the "importance of quality, color and cut" over size. Pictures of "one quarter carat" rings would replace pictures of "up to 2 carat" rings. Moreover, the advertising agency began in its international campaign to "illustrate gems as small as one-tenth of a carat and give them the same emotional importance as larger stones." The news releases also made clear that women should think of diamonds, regardless of size, as objects of perfection: a small diamond could be as perfect as a large diamond.

De Beers devised the "eternity ring," made up of as many as twenty-five tiny Soviet diamonds, which could be sold to an entirely new market of older married women. The advertising campaign was based on the theme of recaptured love. Again, sentiments were born out of necessity: older American women received a ring of miniature diamonds because of the needs of a South African corporation to accommodate the Soviet Union.

The new campaign met with considerable success. The average size of diamonds sold fell from one carat in 1939 to .28 of a carat in 1976, which coincided almost exactly with the average size of the Siberian diamonds De Beers was distributing. However, as American consumers became accustomed to the idea of buying smaller diamonds, they began to perceive larger diamonds as ostentatious. By the mid-1970s, the advertising campaign for smaller diamonds was beginning to seem too successful. In its 1978 strategy report, N. W. Ayer said, "a supply problem has developed... that has had a significant effect on diamond pricing" -- a problem caused by the long-term campaign to stimulate the sale of small diamonds. "Owing to successful pricing, distribution and advertising policies over the last 16 years, demand for small diamonds now appears to have significantly exceeded supply even though supply, in absolute terms, has been increasing steadily." Whereas there was not a sufficient supply of small diamonds to meet the demands of consumers, N. W. Ayer reported that "large stone sales (1 carat and up) ... have maintained the sluggish pace of the last three years." Because of this, the memorandum continued, "large stones are being .. discounted by as much as 20%."

The shortage of small diamonds proved temporary. As Russian diamonds continued to flow into London at an ever-increasing rate, De Beers's strategists came to the conclusion that this production could not be entirely absorbed by "eternity rings" or other new concepts in jewelry, and began looking for markets for miniature diamonds outside the United States. Even though De Beers had met with enormous success in creating an instant diamond "tradition" in Japan, it was unable to create a similar tradition in Brazil, Germany, Austria, or Italy. By paying the high cost involved in absorbing this flood of Soviet diamonds each year, De Beers prevented -- at least temporarily -- the Soviet Union from taking any precipitous actions that might cause diamonds to start glutting the market. N. W. Ayer argued that "small stone jewelry advertising" could not be totally abandoned: "Serious trade relationship problems would ensue if, after fifteen years of stressing 'affordable' small stone jewelry, we were to drop all of these programs."

Instead, the agency suggested a change in emphasis in presenting diamonds to the American public. In the advertisements to appear in 1978, it planned to substitute photographs of one-carat-and-over stones for photographs of smaller diamonds, and to resume both an "informative advertising campaign" and an "emotive program" that would serve to "reorient consumer tastes and price perspectives towards acceptance of solitaire - single-stone - jewelry rather than multi-stone pieces." Other "strategic refinements" it recommended were designed to restore the status of the large diamond. "In fact, this - campaign - will be the exact opposite of the small stone informative program that ran from 1965 to 1970 that popularized the 'beauty in miniature' concept..." With an advertising budget of some $9.69 million, N. W. Ayer appeared confident that it could bring about this "reorientation."

MANIPULATION OF THE DIAMOND MIND

N. W. Ayer learned from an opinion poll it commissioned from the firm of Daniel Yankelovich, Inc. that the gift of a diamond contained an important element of surprise. "Approximately half of all diamond jewelry that the men have given and the women have received were given with zero participation or knowledge on the part of the woman recipient," the study pointed out. N. W Ayer analyzed this "surprise factor":

Women are in unanimous agreement that they want to be surprised with gifts... They want, of course, to be surprised for the thrill of it. However, a deeper, more important reason lies behind this desire... "freedom from guilt." Some of the women pointed out that if their husbands enlisted their help in purchasing a gift (like diamond jewelry), their practical nature would come to the fore and they would be compelled to object to the purchase.

Women were not totally surprised by diamond gifts: some 84 percent of the men in the study "knew somehow" that the women wanted diamond jewelry. The study suggested a two-step "gift-process continuum": first, "the man 'learns' diamonds are o.k." from the woman; then, "at some later point in time, he makes the diamond purchase decision" to surprise the woman.

Through a series of "projective" psychological questions, meant "to draw out a respondent's innermost feelings about diamond jewelry," the study attempted to examine further the semi-passive role played by women in receiving diamonds. The male-female roles seemed to resemble closely the sex relations in a Victorian novel. "Man plays the dominant, active role in the gift process. Woman's role is more subtle, more oblique, more enigmatic..." The woman seemed to believe there was something improper about receiving a diamond gift. Women spoke in interviews about large diamonds as "flashy, gaudy, overdone" and otherwise inappropriate. Yet the study found that "Buried in the negative attitudes... lies what is probably the primary driving force for acquiring them. Diamonds are a traditional and conspicuous signal of achievement, status and success." It was noted, for example, "A woman can easily feel that diamonds are 'vulgar' and still be highly enthusiastic about receiving diamond jewelry." The element of surprise, even if it is feigned, plays the same role of accommodating dissonance in accepting a diamond gift as it does in prime sexual seductions: it permits the woman to pretend that she has not actively participated in the decision. She thus retains both her innocence -- and the diamond.

For advertising diamonds in the late 1970s, the implications of this research were clear. To induce men to buy diamonds for women, advertising should focus on the emotional impact of the "surprise" gift transaction. In the final analysis, a man was moved to part with earnings not by the value, aesthetics, or tradition of diamonds but by the expectation that a "gift of love" would enhance his standing in the eyes of a woman. On the other hand, a woman accepted the gift as a tangible symbol of her status and achievements.

By 1979, N. W. Ayer had helped De Beers expand its sales of diamonds in the United States to more than $2.1 billion, at the wholesale level, compared with a mere $23 million in 1939. In forty years, the value of its sales had increased nearly a hundredfold. The expenditure on advertisements, which began at a level of only $200,000 a year and gradually increased to $10 million, seemed a brilliant investment.

Except for those few stones that have been destroyed, every diamond that has been found and cut into a jewel still exists today and is literally in the public's hands. Some hundred million women wear diamonds, while millions of others keep them in safe-deposit boxes or strongboxes as family heirlooms. It is conservatively estimated that the public holds more than 500 million carats of gem diamonds, which is more than fifty times the number of gem diamonds produced by the diamond cartel in any given year. Since the quantity of diamonds needed for engagement rings and other jewelry each year is satisfied by the production from the world's mines, this half-billion-carat supply of diamonds must be prevented from ever being put on the market. The moment a significant portion of the public begins selling diamonds from this inventory, the price of diamonds cannot be sustained. For the diamond invention to survive, the public must be inhibited from ever parting with its diamonds.

In developing a strategy for De Beers in 1953, N. W. Ayer said: "In our opinion old diamonds are in 'safe hands' only when widely dispersed and held by individuals as cherished possessions valued far above their market price." As far as De Beers and N. W. Ayer were concerned, "safe hands" belonged to those women psychologically conditioned never to sell their diamonds. This conditioning could not be attained solely by placing advertisements in magazines. The diamond-holding public, which includes people who inherit diamonds, had to remain convinced that diamonds retained their monetary value. If it saw price fluctuations in the diamond market and attempted to dispose of diamonds to take advantage of changing prices, the retail market would become chaotic. It was therefore essential that De Beers maintain at least the illusion of price stability.

In the 1971 De Beers annual report, Harry Oppenheimer explained the unique situation of diamonds in the following terms: "A degree of control is necessary for the well-being of the industry, not because production is excessive or demand is falling, but simply because wide fluctuations in price, which have, rightly or wrongly, been accepted as normal in the case of most raw materials, would be destructive of public confidence in the case of a pure luxury such as gem diamonds, of which large stocks are held in the form of jewelry by the general public." During the periods when production from the mines temporarily exceeds the consumption of diamonds -- the balance is determined mainly by the number of impending marriages in the United States and Japan -- the cartel can preserve the illusion of price stability by either cutting back the distribution of diamonds at its London "sights," where, ten times a year, it allots the world's supply of diamonds to about 300 hand-chosen dealers, called "sight-holders," or by itself buying back diamonds at the wholesale level. The underlying assumption is that as long as the general public never sees the price of diamonds fall, it will not become nervous and begin selling its diamonds. If this huge inventory should ever reach the market, even De Beers and all the Oppenheimer resources could not prevent the price of diamonds from plummeting.

THE MONEY FANTASY

A common, if dangerous, assumption is that diamonds retain their value, and, if necessary, can be converted to cash. But selling individual diamonds at a profit, even those held over long periods of time, can be surprisingly difficult. For example, in 1970, the London-based consumer magazine *Money Which?* Decided to test diamonds as a decade long investment. It bought two gem-quality diamonds, weighing approximately one-half carat apiece, from one of London's most reputable diamond dealers, for £400 (then worth about a thousand dollars). For nearly nine years, it kept these two diamonds sealed in an envelope in its vault. During this same period, Great Britain experienced inflation that ran as high as 25 percent a year. For the diamonds to have kept pace with inflation, they would have had to increase in value at least 300 percent, making them worth some £400 pounds by 1978. But when the magazine's editor, Dave Watts, tried to sell the diamonds in 1978, he found that neither jewelry stores nor wholesale dealers in London's Hatton Garden district would pay anywhere near that price for the diamonds. Most of the stores refused to pay any cash for them; the highest bid Watts received was £500, which amounted to a profit of only £100 in over eight years, or less than 3 percent at a compound rate of interest. If the bid were calculated in 1970 pounds, it would amount to only £167. Dave Watts summed up the magazine's experiment by saying, "As an 8-year investment the diamonds that we bought have proved to be very poor." The problem was that the buyer, not the seller, determined the price.

The magazine conducted another experiment to determine the extent to which larger diamonds appreciate in value over a one-year period. In 1970, it bought a 1.42 carat diamond for £745. In 1971, the highest offer it received for the same gem was £568. Rather than sell it at such an enormous loss, Watts decided to extend the experiment until 1974, when he again made the round of the jewelers in Hatton Garden to have it appraised. During this tour of the diamond district, Watts found that the diamond had mysteriously shrunk in weight to 1.04 carats. One of the jewelers had apparently switched diamonds during the appraisal. In that same year, Watts, undaunted, bought another diamond, this one 1.4 carats, from a reputable London dealer. He paid £2,595. A week later, he decided to sell it. The maximum offer he received was £1,000.

In 1976, the Dutch Consumer Association also tried to test the price appreciation of diamonds by buying a perfect diamond of over one carat in Amsterdam, holding it for eight months, and then offering it for sale to the twenty leading dealers in Amsterdam. Nineteen refused to buy it, and the twentieth dealer offered only a fraction of the purchase price.

Selling diamonds can also be an extraordinarily frustrating experience for private individuals. In 1978, for example, a wealthy woman in New York City decided to sell back a diamond ring she had bought from Tiffany two years earlier for $100,000 and use the proceeds toward a necklace of matched pearls that she fancied. She had read about the "diamond boom" in news magazines and hoped that she might make a profit on the diamond. Instead, the sales executive explained, with what she said seemed to be a touch of embarrassment, that Tiffany had "a strict policy against repurchasing diamonds." He assured her, however, that the diamond was extremely valuable, and suggested another Fifth Avenue jewelry store. The woman went from one leading jeweler to another, attempting to sell her diamond. One store offered to swap it for another jewel, and two other jewelers offered to accept the diamond "on consignment" and pay her a percentage of what they sold it for, but none of the half-dozen jewelers she visited offered her cash for her $100,000 diamond. She finally gave up and kept the diamond.

Retail jewelers, especially the prestigious Fifth Avenue stores, prefer not to buy back diamonds from customers, because the offer they would make would most likely be considered ridiculously low. The "keystone," or markup, on a diamond and its setting may range from 100 to 200 percent, depending on the policy of the store; if it bought diamonds back from customers, it would have to buy them back at wholesale prices. Most jewelers would prefer not to make a customer an offer that might be deemed insulting and also might undercut the widely held notion that diamonds go up in value. Moreover, since retailers generally receive their diamonds from wholesalers on consignment, and need not pay for them until they are sold, they would not readily risk their own cash to buy diamonds from customers. Rather than offer customers a fraction of what they paid for diamonds, retail jewelers almost invariably recommend to their clients firms that specialize in buying diamonds "retail."

The firm perhaps most frequently recommended by New York jewelry shops is Empire Diamonds Corporation, which is situated on the sixty-sixth floor of the Empire State Building, in midtown Manhattan. Empire's reception room, which resembles a doctor's office, is usually crowded with elderly women who sit nervously in plastic chairs waiting for their names to be called. One by one, they are ushered into a small examining room, where an appraiser scrutinizes their diamonds and makes them a cash offer. "We usually can't pay more than a maximum of 90 percent of the current wholesale price," says Jack Brod, president of Empire Diamonds. "In most cases we have to pay less, since the setting has to be discarded, and we have to leave a margin for error in our evaluation -- especially if the diamond is mounted in a setting." Empire removes the diamonds from their settings, which are sold as scrap, and resells them to wholesalers. Because of the steep markup on diamonds, individuals who buy retail and in effect sell wholesale often suffer enormous losses. For example, Brod estimates that a half-carat diamond ring, which might cost $2,000 at a retail jewelry store, could be sold for only $600 at Empire.

The appraisers at Empire Diamonds examine thousands of diamonds a month but rarely turn up a diamond of extraordinary quality. Almost all the diamonds they find are slightly flawed, off-color, commercial-grade diamonds. The chief appraiser says, "When most of these diamonds were purchased, American women were concerned with the size of the diamond, not its intrinsic quality." He points out that the setting frequently conceals flaws, and adds, "The sort of flawless, investment-grade diamond one reads about is almost never found in jewelry."

Many of the elderly women who bring their jewelry to Empire Diamonds and other buying services have been victims of burglaries or muggings and fear further attempts. Thieves, however, have an even more difficult time selling diamonds than their victims. When suspicious-looking characters turn up at Empire Diamonds, they are asked to wait in the reception room, and the police are called in. In January of 1980, for example, a disheveled youth came into Empire with a bag full of jewelry that he called "family heirlooms." When Brod pointed out that a few pieces were imitations, the youth casually tossed them into the wastepaper basket. Brod buzzed for the police.

When thieves bring diamonds to underworld "fences," they usually get only a pittance for them. In 1979, for example, New York City police recover stolen diamonds with an insured value of $50,000 which had been sold to a 'fence' for only $200. According to the assistant district attorney who handled the case, the fence was unable to dispose of the diamonds on 47th Street, and he was eventually turned in by one of the diamond dealers he contacted.

While those who attempt to sell diamonds often experience disappointment at the low price they are offered, stories in gossip columns suggest that diamonds are resold at enormous profits. This is because the column items are not about the typical diamond ring that a woman desperately attempts to peddle to small stores and diamond buying services like Empire but about truly extraordinary diamonds that movie stars sell, or claim to sell, in a publicity-charged atmosphere. The legend created around the so-called "Elizabeth Taylor" diamond is a case in point. This pear-shaped diamond, which weighed 69.42 carats after it had been cut and polished, was the fifty-sixth largest diamond in the world and one of the few large-cut diamonds in private hands. Except that it was a diamond, it had little in common with the millions of small stones that are mass-marketed each year in engagement rings and other jewelry.

A serious threat to the stability of the diamond invention came in the late 1970s from the sale of "investment" diamonds to speculators in the United States. A large number of fraudulent investment firms, most of them in Arizona, began telephoning prospective clients drawn from various lists of professionals and investors who had recently sold stock. "Boiler-room operators," many of them former radio and television announcers, persuaded strangers to buy mail-order diamonds as investments that were supposedly much safer than stocks or bonds. Many of the newly created firms also held "diamond-investment seminars" in expensive resort hotels, where they presented impressive graphs and data. Typically assisted by a few well-rehearsed shills in the audience, the seminar leaders sold sealed packets of diamonds to the audience. The leaders often played on the fear of elderly investors that their relatives might try to seize their cash assets and commit them to nursing homes. They suggested that the investors could stymie such attempts by putting their money into diamonds and hiding them.

The sealed packets distributed at these seminars and through the mail included certificates guaranteeing the quality of the diamonds -- as long as the packets remained sealed. Customers who broke the seal often learned from independent appraisers that their diamonds were of a quality inferior to that stated. Many were worthless. Complaints proliferated so fast that, in 1978, the attorney general of New York created a "diamond task force" to investigate the hundreds of allegations of fraud.

Some of the entrepreneurs were relative newcomers to the diamond business. Rayburne Martin, who went from De Beers Diamond Investments, Ltd. (no relation to the De Beers cartel) to Tel-Aviv Diamond Investments, Ltd. -- both in Scottsdale, Arizona -- had a record of embezzlement and securities law violations in Arkansas, and was a fugitive from justice during most of his tenure in the diamond trade. Harold S. McClintock, also known as Harold Sager, had been convicted of stock fraud in Chicago and involved in a silver-bullion-selling caper in 1974 before he helped organize De Beers Diamond Investments, Ltd. Don Jay Shure, who arranged to set up another De Beers Diamond Investments, Ltd., in Irvine, California, had also formerly been convicted of fraud. Bernhard Dohrmann, the Dohrmann, the "marketing director" of the International Diamond Corporation, had served time in jail for security fraud in 1976. Donald Nixon, the nephew of former President Richard M. Nixon, and fugitive financier Robert L. Vesco were, according to the New York State attorney general, participating in the late 1970s in a high-pressure telephone campaign to sell "overvalued or worthless diamonds" by employing "a battery of silken-voiced radio and television announcers." Among the diamond salesmen were also a wide array of former commodity and stock brokers who specialized in attempting to sell sealed diamonds to pension funds and retirement plans.

In London, the real De Beers, unable to stifle all the bogus entrepreneurs using its name, decided to explore the potential market for investment gems. It announced in March of 1978 a highly unusual sort of "diamond fellowship" for selected retail jewelers. Each jeweler who participated would pay a $2,000 fellowship fee. In return, he would receive a set of certificates for investment-grade diamonds, contractual forms for "buy-back" guarantees, promotional material, and training in how to sell these unmounted diamonds to an entirely new category of customers. The selected retailers would then sell loose stones rather than fine jewels, with certificates guaranteeing their value at $4,000 to $6,000.

De Beers's modest move into the investment-diamond business caused a tremor of concern in the trade. De Beers had always strongly opposed retailers selling "investment" diamonds, on the grounds that because customers had no sentimental attachment to such diamonds, they would eventually attempt to resell them and cause sharp price fluctuations.

If De Beers had changed its policy toward investment diamonds, it was not because it wanted to encourage the speculative fever that was sweeping America and Europe. De Beers had "little choice but to get involved," as one De Beers executive explained. Many established diamond dealers had rushed into the investment field to sell diamonds to financial institutions, pension plans, and private investors. It soon became apparent in the Diamond Exchange in New York that selling unmounted diamonds to investors was far more profitable than selling them to jewelry shops. By early 1980, David Birnbaum, a leading dealer in New York, estimated that nearly a third of all diamond sales in the United States were, in terms of dollar value, of these unmounted investment diamonds. "Only five years earlier, investment diamonds were only an insignificant part of the business," he said. Even if De Beers did not approve of this new market in diamonds, it could hardly ignore a third of the American diamond trade.

To make a profit, investors must at some time find buyers who are willing to pay more for their diamonds than they did. Here, however, investors face the same problem as those attempting to sell their jewelry: there is no unified market in which to sell diamonds. Although dealers will quote the prices at which they are willing to sell investment-grade diamonds, they seldom give a set price at which they are willing to buy diamonds of the same grade. In 1977, for example, Jewelers' Circular Keystone polled a large number of retail dealers and found a difference of over 100 percent in offers for the same quality of investment-grade diamonds. Moreover, even though most investors buy their diamonds at or near retail price, they are forced to sell at wholesale prices. As Forbes magazine pointed out, in 1977, "Average investors, unfortunately, have little access to the wholesale market. Ask a jeweler to buy back a stone, and he'll often begin by quoting a price 30% or more below wholesale." Since the difference between wholesale and retail is usually at least 100 percent in investment diamonds, any gain from the appreciation of the diamonds will probably be lost in selling them.

"There's going to come a day when all those doctors, lawyers, and other fools who bought diamonds over the phone take them out of their strongboxes, or wherever, and try to sell them," one dealer predicted last year. Another gave a gloomy picture of what would happen if this accumulation of diamonds were suddenly sold by speculators. "Investment diamonds are bought for $30,000 a carat, not because any woman wants to wear them on her finger but because the investor believes they will be worth $50,000 a carat. He may borrow heavily to leverage his investment. When the price begins to decline, everyone will try to sell their diamonds at once. In the end, of course, there will be no buyers for diamonds at $30,000 a carat or even $15,000. At this point, there will be a stampede to sell investment diamonds, and the newspapers will begin writing stories about the great diamond crash. Investment diamonds constitute, of course, only a small fraction of the diamonds held by the public, but when women begin reading about a diamond crash, they will take their diamonds to retail jewelers to be appraised and find out that they are worth less than they paid for them. At that point, people will realize that diamonds are not forever, and jewelers will be flooded with customers trying to sell, not buy, diamonds. That will be the end of the diamond business."

CONTROLLING ISRAEL

But a panic on the part of investors is not the only event that could end the diamond business. De Beers is at this writing losing control of several sources of diamonds that might flood the market at any time, deflating forever the price of diamonds.

In the winter of 1978, diamond dealers in New York City were becoming increasingly concerned about the possibility of a serious rupture, or even collapse, of the "pipeline" through which De Beers's diamonds flow from the cutting centers in Europe to the main retail markets in America and Japan. This pipeline, a crucial component of the diamond invention, is made up of a network of brokers, diamond cutters, bankers, distributors, jewelry manufacturers, wholesalers, and diamond buyers for retail establishments. Most of the people in this pipeline are Jewish, and virtually all are closely interconnected, through family ties or long-standing business relationships.

An important part of the pipeline goes from London to diamond-cutting factories in Tel Aviv to New York; but in Israel, diamond dealers were stockpiling supplies of diamonds rather than processing and passing them through the pipeline to New York. Since the early 1970s, when diamond prices were rapidly increasing and Israeli currency was depreciating by more than 50 percent a year, it had been more profitable for Israeli dealers to keep the diamonds they received from London than to cut and sell them. As more and more diamonds were taken out of circulation in Tel Aviv, an acute shortage began in New York, driving prices up.

In early 1977, Sir Philip Oppenheimer dispatched his son Anthony to Tel Aviv, accompanied by other De Beers executives, to announce that De Beers intended to cut the Israeli quota of diamonds by at least 20 percent during the coming year. This warning had the opposite effect of what he intended. Rather than paring down production to conform to this quota, Israeli manufacturers and dealers began building up their own stockpiles of diamonds, paying a premium of 100 percent or more for the unopened boxes of diamonds that De Beers shipped to Belgian and American dealers. (By selling their diamonds to the Israelis, the De Beers clients could instantly double their money without taking any risks.) Israeli buyers also moved into Africa and began buying directly from smugglers. The Intercontinental Hotel in Liberia, then the center for the sale of smuggled goods, became a sort of extension of the Israeli bourse. After the Israeli dealers purchased the diamonds, either from De Beers clients or from smugglers, they received 80 percent of the amount they had paid in the form of a loan from Israeli banks. Because of government pressure to help the diamond industry, the banks charged only 6 percent interest on these loans, well below the rate of inflation in Israel. By 1978, the banks had extended $850 million in credit to diamond dealers, an amount equal to some 5 percent of the entire gross national product of Israel. The only collateral the banks had for these loans was uncut diamonds.

De Beers estimated that the Israeli stockpile was more than 6 million carats in 1977, and growing at a rate of almost half a million carats a month. At that rate, it would be only a matter of months before the Israeli stockpile would exceed the cartel's in London. If Israel controlled such an enormous quantity of diamonds, the cartel could no longer fix the price of diamonds with impunity. At any time, the Israelis could be forced to pour these diamonds onto the world market. The cartel decided that it had no alternative but to force liquidation of the Israeli stockpile.

If De Beers wanted to bring the diamond speculation under control, it would have to clamp down on the banks, which were financing diamond purchases with artificially low interest rates. De Beers announced that it was adopting a new strategy of imposing "surcharges" on diamonds. Since these "surcharges," which might be as much as 40 percent of the value of the diamonds, were effectively a temporary price increase, they could pose a risk to banks extending credit to diamond dealers. For example, with a 40 percent surcharge, a diamond dealer would have to pay $1,400 rather than $1,000 for a small lot of diamonds; however, if the surcharge was withdrawn, the diamonds would be worth only a thousand dollars. The Israeli banks could not afford to advance 80 percent of a purchase price that included the so-called surcharge; they therefore required additional collateral from dealers and speculators. Further, they began, under pressure from De Beers, to raise interest rates on outstanding loans.

Within a matter of weeks in the summer of 1978, interest rates on loans to purchase diamonds went up 50 percent. Moreover, instead of lending money based on what Israeli dealers paid for diamonds, the banks began basing their loans on the official De Beers price for diamonds. If a dealer paid more than the De Beers price for diamonds -- and most Israeli dealers were paying at least double the price -- he would have to finance the increment with his own funds.

To tighten the squeeze on Israel, De Beers abruptly cut off shipments of diamonds to forty of its clients who had been selling large portions of their consignments to Israeli dealers. As Israeli dealers found it increasingly difficult either to buy or finance diamonds, they were forced to sell diamonds from the stockpiles they had accumulated. Israeli diamonds poured onto the market, and prices at the wholesale level began to fall. This decline led the Israeli banks to put further pressure on dealers to liquidate their stocks to repay their loans.

Hundreds of Israeli dealers, unable to meet their commitments, went bankrupt as prices continued to plunge. The banks inherited the diamonds.

Last spring, executives of the Diamond Trading Company made an emergency trip to Tel Aviv. They had been informed that three Israeli banks were holding $1.5 billion worth of diamonds in their vaults -- an amount equal to nearly the annual production of all the diamond mines in the world -- and were threatening to dump the hoard of diamonds onto an already depressed market. When the banks had investigated the possibilities of reselling the diamonds in Europe or the United States, they found little interest. The world diamond market was already choked with uncut and unsold diamonds. The only alternative to dumping their diamonds on the market was reselling them to De Beers itself.

De Beers, however, is in no position to absorb such a huge cache of diamonds. During the recession of the mid-1970s, it had to use a large portion of its cash reserve to buy diamonds from Russia and from newly independent countries in Africa, in order to preserve the cartel arrangement. As it added diamonds to its stockpile, De Beers depleted its cash reserves. Furthermore, in 1980, De Beers found it necessary to buy back diamonds on the wholesale markets in Antwerp to prevent a complete collapse in diamond prices. When the Israeli banks approached De Beers about the possibility of buying back the diamonds, De Beers, possibly for the first time since the depression of the 1930s, found itself severely strapped for cash. It could, of course, borrow the $1.5 billion necessary to bail out the Israeli banks, but this would strain the financial structure of the entire Oppenheimer empire.

CARTELS ARE NOT FOREVER

Sir Philip Oppenheimer, Monty Charles, Michael Grantham, and other top executives from De Beers and its subsidiaries attempted to prevent the Israeli banks from dumping their hoard of diamonds. Despite their best efforts, however, the situation worsened. Last September, Israel's major banks quietly informed the Israeli government that they faced losses of disastrous proportions from defaulted accounts almost entirely collateralized with diamonds. Three of Israel's largest banks -- the Union Bank of Israel, the Israel Discount Bank, and Barclays Discount Bank -- had loans of some $660 million outstanding to diamond dealers, which constituted a significant portion of the bank debt in Israel. To be sure, not all of these loans were in jeopardy; but, according to bank estimates, defaults in diamond accounts rose to 20 percent of their loan portfolios. The crisis had to be resolved either by selling the diamonds that had been put up as collateral, which might precipitate a worldwide selling panic, or by some sort of outside assistance from the Israeli government or De Beers or both. The negotiations provided only stopgap assistance: De Beers would buy back a small proportion of the diamonds, and the Israeli government would not force the banks to conform to banking regulations that would result in the liquidation of the stockpile.

"Nobody took into account that diamonds, like any other commodity, can drop in value," Mark Mosevics, chairman of First International Bank of Israel, explained to The New York Times. According to industry estimates, the average one-carat flawless diamond had fallen in value by 50 percent since January of 1980. In March of 1980, for example, the benchmark value for such a diamond was $63,000; in September of 1981, it was only $23,000. This collapse of prices forced Israeli banks to sell diamonds from their stockpile at enormous discounts. One Israeli bank reportedly liquidated diamonds valued at $6 million for $4 million in cash in late 1981. It became clear to the diamond trade that a major stockpile of large diamonds was out of De Beers's control.

The most serious threat to De Beers is yet another source of diamonds that it does not control -- a source so far untapped. Since Cecil Rhodes and the group of European bankers assembled the components of the diamond invention at the end of the nineteenth century, managers of the diamond cartel have shared a common nightmare -- that a giant new source of diamonds would be discovered outside their purview. Sir Ernest Oppenheimer, using all the colonial connections of the British Empire, succeeded in weaving the later discoveries of diamonds in Africa into the fabric of the cartel; Harry Oppenheimer managed to negotiate a secret agreement that effectively brought the Soviet Union into the cartel. However, these brilliant efforts did not end the nightmare. In the late 1970s, vast deposits of diamonds were discovered in the Argyle region of Western Australia, near the town of Kimberley (coincidentally named after Kimberley, South Africa). Test drillings last year indicated that these pipe mines could produce up to 50 million carats of diamonds a year -- more than the entire production of the De Beers cartel in 1981. Although only a small percentage of these diamonds are of gem quality, the total number produced would still be sufficient to change the world geography of diamonds. Either these 50 million carats would be brought under control or the diamond invention would be destroyed.

De Beers rapidly moved to get a stranglehold on the Australian diamonds. It began by acquiring a small, indirect interest in Conzinc Rio Tinto of Australia, Ltd. (CRA), the company that controlled most of the mining rights. In 1980, it offered a secret deal to CRA through which it would market the total output of Australian production. This agreement might have ended the Australian threat if Northern Mining Corporation, a minority partner in the venture, had accepted the deal. Instead, Northern Mining leaked the terms of the deal to a leading Australian newspaper, which reported that De Beers planned to pay the Australian consortium 80 percent less than the existing market price for the diamonds. This led to a furor in Australia. The opposition Labour Party charged not only that De Beers was seeking to cheat Australians out of the true value of the diamonds but that the deal with De Beers would support the policy of apartheid in South Africa. It demanded that the government impose export controls on the diamonds rather than allow them to be controlled by a South African corporation. Prime Minister Malcolm Fraser, faced with a storm of public protest, said that he saw no advantage in "arrangements in which Australian diamond discoveries only serve to strengthen a South African monopoly." He left the final decision on marketing, however, to the Western Australia state government and the mining companies, which may or may not decide to make an arrangement with De Beers.

De Beers also faces a crumbling empire in Zaire. Sir Ernest Oppenheimer had concluded, more than fifty years ago, that control over the diamond mines in Zaire (then called the Belgian Congo) was the key to the cartel's control of world production. De Beers, together with its Belgian partners, had instituted mining and sorting procedures that would maximize the production of industrial (rather than gem) diamonds. Since there was no other ready customer for the enormous quantities of industrial diamonds the Zairian mines produced, De Beers remained their only outlet. In June of last year, however, President Mobuto abruptly announced that his country's exclusive contract with a De Beers subsidiary would not be renewed. Mobuto was reportedly influenced by offers he received for Zaire's diamond production from both Indian and American manufacturers. According to one New York diamond dealer, "Mobuto simply wants a more lucrative deal." Whatever his motives, the sudden withdrawal of Zaire from the cartel further undercuts the stability of the diamond market. With increasing pressure for the independence of Namibia, and a less friendly government in neighboring Botswana, De Beers's days of control in black Africa seem numbered.

How long can De Beers's executives maneuver to save the diamond invention by buying up loose diamonds? The swelling inventory of diamonds in De Beers's vault can only be financed so long as De Beers can make a profit selling the diamonds from its own mines.

The most serious threat to De Beers is yet another source of diamonds that it does not control -- a source so far untapped. Since Cecil Rhodes and the group of European bankers assembled the components of the diamond invention at the end of the nineteenth century, managers of the diamond cartel have shared a common nightmare -- that a giant new source of diamonds would be discovered outside their purview. Sir Ernest Oppenheimer, using all the colonial connections of the British Empire, succeeded in weaving the later discoveries of diamonds in Africa into the fabric of the cartel; Harry Oppenheimer managed to negotiate a secret agreement that effectively brought the Soviet Union into the cartel. However, these brilliant efforts did not end the nightmare. In the late 1970s, vast deposits of diamonds were discovered in the Argyle region of Western Australia, near the town of Kimberley (coincidentally named after Kimberley, South Africa). Test drillings last year indicated that these pipe mines could produce up to 50 million carats of diamonds a year -- more than the entire production of the De Beers cartel in 1981. Although only a small percentage of these diamonds are of gem quality, the total number produced would still be sufficient to change the world geography of diamonds. Either these 50 million carats would be brought under control or the diamond invention would be destroyed.

De Beers also faces a crumbling empire in Zaire. Sir Ernest Oppenheimer had concluded, more than fifty years ago, that control over the diamond mines in Zaire (then called the Belgian Congo) was the key to the cartel's control of world production. De Beers, together with its Belgian partners, had instituted mining and sorting procedures that would maximize the production of industrial (rather than gem) diamonds. Since there was no other ready customer for the enormous quantities of industrial diamonds the Zairian mines produced, De Beers remained their only outlet. In June of last year, however, President Mobuto abruptly announced that his country's exclusive contract with a De Beers subsidiary would not be renewed. Mobuto was reportedly influenced by offers he received for Zaire's diamond production from both Indian and American manufacturers. According to one New York diamond dealer, "Mobuto simply wants a more lucrative deal." Whatever his motives, the sudden withdrawal of Zaire from the cartel further undercuts the stability of the diamond market. With increasing pressure for the independence of Namibia, and a less friendly government in neighboring Botswana, De Beers's days of control in black Africa seem numbered.

Even in the midst of this crisis, De Beers's executives in London have been maneuvering to save the diamond invention by buying up loose diamonds. The swelling inventory of diamonds in De Beers's vault needs to be financed out of its profits. Yet, as avalanche of diamonds from new discoveries in Australian, Canada, and elsewhere pour onto the market, there is a limit to how many of them De Beers can buy up and stockpile. Unless it can find an affordable way to gain control of the various sources of diamonds that threaten to crowd the market, these sources may bring about the final collapse of world diamond prices. If they do, the diamond invention will disintegrate and be remembered only as a historical curiosity, as brilliant in its way as the glittering little stones it once made so valuable.

-- *This essay appeared in the Atlantic in February 1982*

***

II

The Mystery of the Russian Diamonds

Every month, at a time which is a closely guarded secret, an Aeroflot jet will touch down in London, with over one million diamonds on board. As it arrives, somewhere between $50 million and $100 million, will be transferred by wire into a Moscow account.

From the airport, the Russian diamonds are whisked across London to number 2 Charterhouse Street, headquarters of De Beers' Diamond trading Company. There they are added to the glut of unsalable diamonds now swelling the four-story deep vault.

This monthly transaction is part of a secret deal struck between De Beers and the Soviet Union in 1962. And it is now, twenty years later, causing the western world's diamond cartel, as well as its intelligence services, increasing anxiety since there is growing evidence that not all these gem-quality diamonds, if they are mined at all in Siberia, are not produced by conventional means.

De Beers does not welcome these expensive parcels from Moscow -- and yet it has little choice but to accept them. If it pulled out of the deal, the Russians, who in 1981 already supplied one quarter of all the world's gem diamonds, might well flood the market and, in doing so, could the price of diamonds to plunge.

When the Russians discovered a Kimberlite diamond "pipe" at Mirney in Siberia in 1955, it was assumed by De Beers engineer that this rich mine, like similar "pipes" in Southern Africa, would produce well for 5-10 years, then gradually decline.

So, in 1962, De Beers had little hesitation in agreeing to buy virtually all the uncut diamonds produced by the Soviet Union. And for the first 10 years, production from the Mirney mine was much as De Beers had expected.

But then, just as production from Mirney was expected to level off on 1970, an odd thing happened. To the dismay and shock of the diamond cartel, the size of Russian shipments to London increased.

Between 1970 and 1975 Siberian diamond production increased from 10 million carats to 16 million, leading De Beers geologists to wonder how the Siberian pipe could produce roughly 5 times as many diamonds as comparable pipes in South Africa.

Adding to the mystery was the lack of Siberian industrial diamonds. Based on the huge production of gem-quality diamonds, De beers assumed Russia would have an excess of industrial diamonds (since mines normally yield both types.) And yet, Russia was increasing its orders for Industrial diamonds from the West.

De Beers sorters in London also noticed that the more recent diamonds shipped from Russia had some extraordinary aspects. For one thing, they tended to have a greenish tint and sharp angular edges, which differentiated them from most other diamonds in the De Beers vault.

Secondly, the Siberian diamonds were remarkably uniform both in size and shape. The vast preponderance of them weighed just under a quarter of a carat. Whereas diamonds from De Beers own mines came in a multitude of shapes -- round, square, oblong, flat, triangular, and twisted -- the Siberian diamonds were mainly a single shape, octahedron.

As suspicions grew, De Beers decided to investigate. Sir Philip Oppenheimer, then managing director of the Diamond Trading Company, and Barry Hawthorne, chief geologist for De Beers in Kimberley, asked to visit the Siberian mine.

Although after some hassle permission was eventually granted, their party was so delayed at the airport that when it finally arrived, it had less than an hour to inspect the mines. Even so, what Hawthorne saw there convinced him that the Mirney mine was incapable of producing anywhere near the number of diamonds that were being shipped to London. As far as he could determine, the hole in the ground was far too small, and the mine lacked the facilities necessary to extract and sort, that large a quantity of diamonds.

If not that mine, where were the Russian diamonds pouring into De Beers vault coming from?

One ominous possibility is that the Russians were making them in hydraulic presses. In June 1982, a spokesman for the Institute of High Pressure Physics in Moscow conformed to the Sunday Times of London that Soviet scientists had succeeded in synthesizing gem-quality diamonds weighing up to half a carat out of carbon. The process was developed in the 1960s by Moscow scientist Leonid Vereschyagin, who headed a staff of 1200 researchers. The process involved putting carbon "seeds" in hydraulic presses and through the application of heat and pressure growing them into diamonds.

There was not no doubt Russians had produced some man-made diamonds. They were first observed by Western scientists in the late 1960s -- about the time production at the Siberian mines were expected to start declining. Their shape and greenish-tint was not unlike the diamonds that began arriving in London in the 1970s. The issue was did they have the means to mass produce them. If so, could the diamonds De Beers was buying from Russia come from hydraulic presses?

Wherever they come from, they are Russia's chief earner of hard currency. So Russia is not likely to cut back on their production, but this poses an immense dilemma for De Beers. Either it must continue to buy from Russia to keep them off the market, which costs it over $1 billion a year, or see them released onto the fragile market and possibly destroy the illusion that diamonds are forever.

-- *This article was published by the Sunday Times - London - on June 20, 1982*

***

III

Blood Diamonds

De Beers announced with great fanfare in July 2000 that it was abandoning its policy of buying diamonds in African conflict zones, occasioning both applause and predictions of De Beers' demise. But the diamond cartel, while modifying its tactics, has not changed its basic strategy. Almost since its inception at the end of the 19th century, the diamond cartel has had a singular strategy: stifling, by any means necessary, the flow of gem diamonds from sources not under its ownership or control.

The problem with diamonds isn't their scarcity, but their abundance. They are found not only in geological formations like volcanic pipes that can be fenced off and mined, but also in vast alluvial areas like river beds or beaches, places that can't be restricted. When Europe ruled Africa, the cartel had little problem making arrangements with colonial administrators to police or close down freelance diamond gathering. After African colonies got their independence, the cartel came to terms with dictators like Mobutu Sese Seko, whose police kept out -- and occasionally massacred -- suspected smugglers. Where governments were less cooperative or capable, the cartel commissioned mercenaries to suppress, often by maiming or killing, prospective diamond hunters. At one point in the 1960s, the cartel gave bounties to remnants of the Katanga gendarmerie to hunt down "smugglers" in Angola. It also paid a Lebanese mercenary named Fred Kamil in Sierra Leone to arrange ambushes that would persuade Mandago tribesman to quit the diamond trade. Since these measures didn't fully eliminate the "leakage" to diamond-cutting centers in Belgium, Israel and India, it also acted as a buyer of last resort to keep prices from falling.

But that is history. The cartel now has found an ingenious new mechanism for achieving its ends: the United Nations. After spending months laying the conceptual groundwork in the media, as well as working through human-rights communities, it has convinced the U.N. Security Council to impose a global ban on "undocumented" gem diamonds from "conflict zones." Undocumented diamonds are, of course, just those diamonds picked out of river beds that De Beers wants eliminated. The "conflict zones," Angola and Sierra Leone, are the alluvial areas in which De Beers previously depended on paid guns.

Instead of using colonial administrations, dictators or mercenary gangs to stop Africans from gathering and selling stones, the U.N. will use its resources (backed, no doubt, by the cartel's own contingent of lawyers and detectives) to accomplish that task. The cartel managed this favorable outcome by playing on the guilt of the West. The idea that "blood diamonds" were responsible for ferocious civil wars in Africa was too much for altruists and activists in developed nations. President Bill Clinton then called for "an international conference to consider practical approaches to breaking the link between the illicit trade in diamonds and armed conflict..." President Clinton stated at a May conference in South Africa, the U.S., Britain and Belgium, among others, had agreed with De Beers upon the importance of establishing a global certification scheme for diamonds. De Beers was thus empowered to create a regime, which would include stamping identification marks on diamonds, which would aim to stamp out unauthorized sales of diamonds.

Like all persuasive ideas, the concept of blood diamonds is not without a basis in reality. Diamonds, like any resource, can be converted to money. Money can be used to buy arms and ammunition. What the concept neglects, however, is that governments are the principal means by which warriors get funded and armed. Countries such as the Sudan, Ethiopia, Somalia, Rwanda, Burundi and Liberia have managed to sustain ferocious civil wars for years without having or selling diamonds. Even countries rich in diamonds have found alternative ways to finance their warfare: In Angola, Unita rebels were armed by the Central Intelligence Agency, South Africa's intelligence service and Zaire. In the Congo, at least seven African governments are presently intervening in the civil war with arms and troops. A regime backed by the U.N. and U.S. that inhibits the sale of uncertified diamonds, diamonds that in practice come from fields the cartel doesn't control, probably won't stop civil wars, then. It will, however, make it far less costly for De Beers to control the diamond market. It was another brilliant coup for the cartel.

-- *This article appeared in the Wall Street Journal on August 3, 2000*

***

IV

DE BEER'S NIGHTMARE SCENARIO

Responding to the global recession in 2009, the De Beers diamond cartel has cut back production at its South African mines and reduced the price of its rough diamonds between 15 and 20 percent. Even so, industry sources in South Africa are now estimating that diamond prices could fall another "59-63 percent." But the real fear of the diamond cartel is not just that retail prices will decline - it has managed that problem before - but that the public will begin to sell its hoard of diamonds, or what is called at De Beers "the overhang."

At the heart of this concern is the reality that, except for those few stones that have been permanently lost, every diamond that has been found and cut into a gem since the beginning of time still exists today. This enormous inventory, which overhangs the market, is literally in - or on - the public's hands. Some hundred million women wear diamonds, while millions of other people keep them in safe deposit boxes as family heirlooms.

De Beers executives estimate that the public holds more than 500 million carats of gem diamonds, which is more than 50 times the number of gem diamonds produced by the diamond cartel in any given year. The moment a significant portion of the public begins selling diamonds from this prodigious inventory, the cartel would be unable to sustain the price of diamonds, or maintain the illusion that they are such a rare stone that their value is, as the ad slogan claims, "forever."

As Harry Oppenheimer, who headed the cartel for more than a quarter of a century, pointed out, "wide fluctuations in price, which have, rightly or wrongly, been accepted as normal in the case of most raw materials, would be destructive of public confidence in the case of a pure luxury such as gem diamonds, of which large stocks are held in the form of jewelry by the general public."

The genius of the cartel was creating this "confidence" in the myth that the value of diamonds was eternal. In developing a strategy for De Beers in 1952, the advertising agency N.W. Ayer noted in a report to De Beers: "Diamonds do not wear out and are not consumed. New diamonds add to the existing supply in trade channels and in the possession of the public. In our opinion old diamonds are in 'safe hands' only when widely dispersed and held by individuals as cherished possessions valued far above their market price."

In other words, for the diamond illusion to survive, the public must be psychologically inhibited from ever parting with their diamonds. The advertising agency's basic assignment was to make women value diamonds as permanent possessions, not for their actual worth on the market. It set out to accomplish this task by attempting through subtly designed advertisements to foster a sentimental attachment to diamonds that would make it difficult for a woman to give them up. Women were induced to think of diamonds as their "best friends."

This conditioning could not be attained solely by magazine advertisements. The diamond-holding public, which included individuals who inherited diamonds, had to remain convinced that the gems retained their monetary value. If they attempted to take advantage of changing prices, the retail market would be chaotic.

Even during the Great Depression of the 1930s, there was only a limited overhang, since the mass-marketing of diamonds had begun only a single generation before the crash. So even though demand for diamonds almost completely abated, De Beers, by shuttering all its mines and borrowing money to buy up the production of the small number of independent mines that still existed, was able to weather the crisis.

Today, however, with many generations of the diamonds it mass-marketed overhanging the market, and most of global diamond production in independent hands, it no longer is in a position to bring supply and demand into balance. Adding to this precarious situation, diamond cutters, manufacturers and dealers, have, as of Feb. 15 2009, an estimated $40 to $50 billion worth of diamonds in mines in the pipeline that will intensify the downward spiral when the gems reach the market later this year.

If falling prices shatter the carefully nurtured illusion that the value of the glittering stones kept in jewel boxes and vaults is eternal, and the public begins selling even part of its hoard, De Beer's nightmare scenario would come true: These stockpiled diamonds, which hang

over the diamond market like the sword of Damocles, would suddenly cascade into the market.

*-- This article appeared in the International Herald Tribune on Decem-
ber 3, 2009*

***

V

THE END OF THE CARTEL

For over a century, the De Beers cartel succeeded, despite the great depression, a half dozen recessions, and vast new discovery of diamonds pipes in Australia and Siberia, to prevent the massive overhang in jewel boxes, vaults, and investment funds from flooding onto the diamond market. This incredible achievement in itself made it the most successful cartel in history. It also proved brilliantly adaptable to political change. When civil war and chaos in West and Central Africa opened up diamond fields it had previously controlled through arrangements with politicians and warlords in the 1990s, De Beers brilliantly exploited the outcry against so-called "blood diamonds" to get human-rights organizations, European governments, and the U.N. Security Council to impose a global ban on "undocumented" gem diamonds from "conflict zones" in 2000. Such undocumented diamonds included those diamonds picked out of river beds By Africans and sold into markets outside of the cartel's purview. The "conflict zones" specified in the UN resolution including the alluvial areas in Congo, Angola and Sierra Leone that De Beers had previously controlled by its network of buying-agents and mercenary gangs.

Now, to prevent these diamonds from financing civil strife, the UN had been induced to do the job for De Beers. With De Beers assistance, it established a global certification regime for diamonds that effectively accomplished De Beers' century-long goal of stifling the flow of gem diamonds to markets it did not control.

In 2005, De Beers also managed to settle the anti-trust that the US government had instituted in 1945 by agreeing to pay $295 million back to diamond purchasers and consenting to abide by an injunction that prohibits it from monopolizing the world supply of rough diamonds. Even if this injunction is difficult, if not impossible, to enforce by a US court, De Beers had also contend with demands from the European Commission, the European Union's anti-trust arm, that it end it deal to buy diamonds from Russia for its stockpile. This arrangement had been a key element in the cartel structure for nearly half a century. Without it, De Beers could not keep the flood of Russian diamonds off the market and control the price of diamonds. Yet, to abide by the new anti-trust laws of the European Union, De Beers had to terminate it by 2009. The solution De Beers found was to effectively relinquished control over the diamond prices to the Russia's state-controlled monopoly, Alrosa, which was also the world's largest diamond producer. Since Russia was not a member of the European Union, it was not bound by its anti-trust rules. In one of the great ironies of History, Vladimir Putin's Russia now assumed control over what had been a symbol of capitalism, the diamond cartel. The Russian diamond monopoly's spokesman made it clear Russia meant to limit supply. "If you don't support the price," he told the New York Times, "a diamond becomes a mere piece of carbon."

But while the Russians may share the motivation of De Beers, the diamond invention is far more than a crude monopoly for fixing diamond prices; it is a mechanism for converting tiny crystals of carbon into universally recognized tokens of wealth, power, and romance. De Beers managed this feat through its brilliant organizational efforts. For three generations, the Oppenheimer family built a network of relationships with diamond cutters in Antwerp, brokers in Tel Aviv, intermediaries in Africa, and bankers in London based on a mutual trust. This network furnished, among other things, much of the pricing intelligence, discipline and public relations that allowed De Beers to control the diamond trade. If the Russian monopoly lacks the necessary human capital to run this delicate mechanism, the illusion at the heart of the diamond invention, along with the diamond prices it has for so long sustained, may be forever shattered.

The diamond invention is neither eternal nor self-perpetuating. It survived for the past century because two critical conditions were satisfied: the production of diamonds from the world's mines was kept in balance with world consumption; and the public refrained from attempting to sell its inventory back onto the market. But De Beers is in the process of changing its strategy to conform to anti-trust laws. Instead of attempting to control the supply of diamonds, it is aiming to brand the name De Beers and sell diamonds directly into the retail market. If this is the end of the cartel, De Beers' previous achievements may prove to be temporary phenomena. The diamond craze of the twentieth century could end as abruptly in the twenty-first century as the tulip mania of the eighteenth century. If that ever happens, the diamond invention will disintegrate and be remembered only as a historical curiosity, as brilliant in its way as the glittering, brittle, little stones it once made so valuable.

***

VI

THE OPPENHEIMER EXIT

The first Oppenheimer to share the diamond cartel was Ernest Oppenheimer came to Kimberley, South Africa in 1902 to run the buying office of Dunkelsbuhler, a member of the London syndicate that controlled diamond sales. He was in many ways the prototype of the multinational businessman: German by birth, British by naturalization, Jewish by religion, and South African by residence.

Oppenheimer's initial success in acquiring capital came, however, from gold rather than diamond mines. A group of German investors, who were clients of Dunkelsbuhler, wanted to invest in gold properties in the Transvaal, and Oppenheimer arranged for them to buy an interest in operating gold mines. In making these deals, he took for himself a small percentage of the venture, as well as an option to increase his participation at a future date.

By 1914, the outbreak of the First World War made the German investment increasingly precarious: Germany was, after all, now an enemy of the British Commonwealth. As the pressure mounted on the government for the expropriation of enemy assets in South Africa, Oppenheimer found a solution for the German investors. He personally created an international corporation in which the German interest could be subtly diffused with those of investors of other nationalities including him. To avoid drawing any unnecessary attention to the German investments, he proposed giving the corporation a name that would strongly suggest an "American connection," as Oppenheimer put it. In a letter to his associates, he wrote, "Our aim should be for our company to make its debut as a new factor in South African finance." After considering the name United South Africa Company, which would be abbreviated USA Company, and then the Afro-American Company, they finally decided on the Anglo-American Corporation, which sounded very much like the Anglo-American alliance that was then winning the war. The mask seemed to work at least with the South African press: when the new corporation was announced in September 1917, the Rand Daily Mail proclaimed in a headline, "American Millions for the Rand."

After establishing his corporation, Oppenheimer quickly shifted his attention from gold back to diamonds. As early as 1910, he had concluded in a memorandum that "the only way to increase the value of diamonds is to make them scarce, that is, to reduce production." He believed that De Beers could bring about such scarcity but only if it expanded its reach beyond the borders of South Africa. He viewed control of the South African mines as a necessary, but not sufficient, condition for an effective diamond monopoly.

After Rhodes' death, the management of De Beers had based its monopoly on the proposition that there would not be new major discoveries of diamonds. When a bricklayer named Thomas M. Cullinan claimed to have discovered diamonds in a huge oval of yellow dirt some 600 miles north of Kimberley, De Beers's geologists scoffed at the idea of diamond pipes existing outside of the Kimberley area. Frank Oats, who had succeeded Rhodes as head of De Beers, went so far as to declare that "the whole thing was a fake."

It quickly turned out Oats had been wrong: The Premier was a diamond pipe, larger than any other found in the world, and four times the size of Kimberley's Big Hole mine. When the news was conveyed to Alfred Beit, who along with Rhodes and Barnato been a life governor of De Beers, he had a heart attack from which he never recovered.

Cullinan himself was prepared to fight another diamond war rather than sell out to De Beers. To raise capital for this mine, he sold a majority interest to the Transvaal government. Fortunately for De Beers, the British had just triumphed over the Boer settlers in the Transvaal in the Boer War, and they were able to pressure the Transvaal into coming to terms with De Beers.

Before Oppenheimer could achieve this world monopoly, he first, of course, had to get control of De Beers. The device he used to win a dominant position in De Beers was to acquire a diamond property for Anglo-American that De Beers desperately needed to maintain its monopoly. He then offered to exchange the property for a substantial number of shares in De Beers itself. This property was in the German colony of South-West Africa (now Namibia).

With the German investors in a state of near panic, Oppenheimer saw the possibility of staging his coup. He had personally assessed the various German properties in the forbidden zone on behalf of the London syndicate, and working through his network of cousins in

Germany, he offered each of the major German investor's shares in the Anglo-American Corporation for their holdings in the Namibian diamond beach It was a deal they found difficult to reject. Since most of these Germans fully expected their assets to be appropriated by the allies for the duration of the war, they had little hope of receiving any income from them. The Oppenheimer exchange provided them with a liquid asset. Those who preferred not to accept Anglo-American stock received a cash payment. In the end, Oppenheimer acquired almost all of the German properties, which he reorganized into company called Consolidated Diamond Mines.

Oppenheimer had perceived from the beginning, De Beers, could not afford to wage a diamond war against his Consolidated Diamond Mines. The beaches of Namibia held far too many diamonds for competition to prove anything but ruinous. Nor did Oppenheimer have any intention of competing with De Beers. Instead, Oppenheimer offered the Namibian diamond to De Beers in return for a large block of stock. He was immediately given a place on the board of directors. At every opportunity, he bought more shares of De Beers. So did his cousins. By 1927, he had become the most powerful force in the diamond monopoly. He appealed to Lord Rothschild, whose bank still owned a large block of stock in De Beers, to support his candidacy, and in 1929 Oppenheimer became chairman of the board of De Beers. He was then knighted by the king of England for his services to the British Empire.

Oppenheimer wanted to create a truly international business that owed its allegiance to no single nation. His strategy, he explained to his brother Louis in a letter, was to make De Beers "the absolute controlling factor in the diamond world." By "absolute," he meant control of each and every link in the diamond chain that led from the mines to the distribution network for diamonds. He reasoned that "the danger to the security of the diamond industry is not the discovery of a new rich diamond field, but the irrational exploitation of it." If De Beers could choke off the "irrational" sale of diamonds before they reached the retail market, it could contain any temporary oversupply of diamonds that developed from new mines. It was imperative to prevent at all costs the retail price of diamonds from falling. When all the complicated exchanges of stock were completed, Oppenheimer's Anglo-American Corporation emerged as the controlling shareholder in De Beers.

In 1929, the onslaught of the worldwide Depression strained the ability of the syndicate in London to continue to absorb the world's diamond production. Since the public virtually stopped buying diamonds, the syndicate had to retain almost all the diamonds mined in the world. By 1931, it was oil the verge of bankruptcy, and cabled its office in Kimberley "No sale possible. Best offers for small quantities were well below cost price. Market quite demoralized. Inform Sir Ernest Oppenheimer."

Oppenheimer immediately understood the gravity of the situation. The syndicate could no longer afford to keep its stockpile intact, and if it placed even a small portion of the diamonds on the market, the price would totally collapse. He further realized that this could forever destroy the public's trust in diamonds as a store of value. He had only one alternative: to now take over the syndicate.

Since Oppenheimer and his relatives owned shares in leading members of the syndicate, there was little resistance to the takeover. The subsequent exchange of stock in fact enhanced, rather than diluted, Oppenheimer's control of the monopoly. He put his younger brother Otto in command of the distribution arm in London, which was now called the Diamond Corporation. He then created the Diamond Trading Company, which took over the responsibility of the syndicate for allocating diamonds to manufacturers and wholesalers.

World sales had fallen to practically nothing- a mere $100,000 worth in 1932- and Oppenheimer next moved to curtail the supply of diamonds. One by one, he closed all major mines in South Africa. Production fell from 2,242,000 carats in 1930 to 14,000 carats in 1933. Prices were plunging. Oppenheimer was able to close down his own mines, but he could not prevent newly discovered diamond mines in the Belgian Congo and Portuguese Angola from continuing to produce diamonds. Even though there was no market for these diamonds, De Beers had to continue buying them up through its Diamond Corporation in London to prevent them from being dumped on the market. To finance these diamonds, De Beers issued bonds.

By 1937, De Beers' stockpile of diamonds had grown to some forty million carats. It was, even in re-Depression times, nearly twenty years' supply. Oppenheimer's empire, which had invested millions of dollars in borrowed money in taking these diamonds off the market, was now itself on the verge of bankruptcy. It had been alleged in the anti-trust suit against De Beers that Oppenheimer had even considering dumping several tons of these diamonds into the North Sea to prevent them from reaching the market.

Oppenheimer was saved from having to implement this radical solution to the oversupply problem by the invention of the diamond grinding wheel. In essence, the wheel was a metal-grinding surface impregnated with crushed diamond powder that permitted a quantum leap in the mass production of automobiles, airplanes and machinery. Steel dies and machine tools had always been used to cut precision parts for industry. As steel blades had to be constantly honed or changed, the production of standardized parts moved at a slow pace. In the early 1930s, the Krupp Company in Germany developed a tungsten carbide alloy that was far more resistant to wear than steel. Before tungsten carbide dies and blades could be adopted by industry, however, some means had to be found for shaping them. Diamonds proved to be the only material hard enough, and the diamond grinding wheel thus became an indispensable tool for mass production.

Instead of jettisoning the small and poorly crystallized diamonds, called boart, into the sea, De Beers began crushing them into powder and supplying them to the automotive, aircraft and machine tool industry. With Europe rearming for war, millions of tons of this powder could be profitably each year. Oppenheimer immediately saw the potential of "Industrial diamonds."

Oppenheimer realized that controlling this vital supply of industrial diamonds was necessary to protect the power of his cartel. Oppenheimer negotiated what amounted to a private treaty with the Belgian government. In return for guaranteeing that the Forminiere Mines would sell all its boart to a De Beers subsidiary in London called the Industrial Diamond Corporation, Oppenheimer agreed to provide the Belgian cutting industry with the lion's share of diamonds from all of De Beers' mines. London would have a complete monopoly on the distribution of diamond powder, and Antwerp, which employed some 20,000 cutters, would remain the preeminent center for cutting diamonds. With the completion of this arrangement with the Belgians, De Beers became an international cartel. He then passed the torch to his son Garry.

Harry Oppenheimer was forty-nine years old when he succeeded his father as chairman of both De Beers and the Anglo-American

Corporation in 1957. A shy, quiet man formerly in the background of the diamond cartel, he was now in sole command of it. It was a position that he had been prepared for all his life.

He explained to me, "I first wanted to be an engine driver, then an admiral - nothing less! - in the Royal Navy and then an ambassador." He added wistfully, "However, all these ambitions had to be abandoned before the age of twelve in favor of a business career."

He went to Charterhouse School in England, and then was admitted to Christ Church College at Oxford. At Oxford, he took his degree in politics, philosophy and economics.

He returned to South Africa in 1929, the year the worldwide Depression began, and went to work at the De Beers sorting house in Kimberley. During this apprenticeship, he learned to separate and evaluate diamonds in their uncut form. He then moved to Johannesburg where he became his father's personal assistant in running the corporate empire. In "deviling" for his father, as he called it, he did everything from ghostwriting speeches to going on secret missions to New York for his father. Although his public role remained minimal during this period, his father had him appointed to the De Beers board of directors in 1937-when he was only twenty-nine.

In 1942, Harry served at the Coastal Command in Cape Town, which had been set up to guard against Japanese infiltration. Here he met Bridget McCall, a young officer in the Women's Auxiliary Army Service, who he married in a military ceremony on March 6; 1943. On June 8th 1945, his son Nicholas Oppenheimer was born.

After the war Harry Oppenheimer entered politics, funding the anti-apartheid Progressive party. He won a seat in 1948 in Parliament, when his father died in 1957; he withdrew entirely from South African politics and concentrated his energies on planning out a new future for the diamond cartel. He recognized that the geopolitical forces in Africa were rapidly changing, and that the problems he would confront in his efforts to preserve the diamond invention would be very different from the ones that his father had faced in colonial Africa. Whereas Sir Ernest had only to worry about economic changes, Harry Oppenheimer realized even as early as 1958, he has written, that he would have to prepare himself for violent political changes. A decade of apartheid under the Nationalist government had served to alienate

South Africa from the rest of the Commonwealth. By 1961, South Africa was formally expelled from the Commonwealth and became a republic. As British colonies, such as Sierra Leone, Ghana and Tanzania, achieved their independence, they severed diplomatic relations with South Africa. Belgium also relinquished control of the Congo, with its vast reserves of diamonds. As these newly independent nations grew increasingly hostile to South Africa, De Beers, which was, after all, a South African corporation, could not openly control their diamond fields. By the mid-1960s, South Africa became a pariah nation.

To keep control over the world supply of diamonds, Harry Oppenheimer made covert arrangements with the governments of Soviet Union, Angola, and other diamond-producing nations to buy up their production. As early as 1964, Oppenheimer informed investors in his company that the "political situation in Africa has created new problems for our group...

There are obvious political objections to the purchase of production from African states." He further reported, "This unfortunate state of affairs has necessitated a considerable reorganization of the group's activities... - diamond - buying operations in the newly independent African states are now, in every case, undertaken by companies registered and managed outside the Republic of South Africa, and which are not subsidiaries of De Beers."

In fact, however, these companies were created and controlled by Oppenheimer for the purpose of serving as intermediaries in the diamond arrangements. In other words, a complicated system of corporate fronts had been set up to obscure the movement of diamonds to De Beers from African states pledged to the destruction of South Africa.

Harry Oppenheimer's strategy was not aimed at deceiving the African governments themselves. They were fully aware that De Beers was the ultimate operator of their mines and marketer of their diamonds. It was intended merely to provide a necessary cloak of "denability" for African politicians.

The ever-expanding number of diamonds coming out of the Soviet Union proved to be an even more vexing challenge. His father had only to concern himself with restricting and allocating the production of the diamond mines in Africa; Harry had to find ways to prevent the Soviets from flooding the world market with their diamonds. He therefore moved to bring the Soviet Union into the cartel arrangement, since, as he eloquently put it, "a single channel ... is in the interest of all diamond producers whatever the political difference between them may be."

Oppenheimer needed a tight-knit staff that could discreetly direct all the operations of the mines, the diamond buyers, and the distribution network from South Africa. He located his headquarters, as had his father, in the Anglo-American Building at 44 Main Street in Johannesburg. In theory, Anglo-American and De Beers are two separate entities; in fact, the Oppenheimers, who then owned a controlling interest in both companies, treated them as a single empire, Anglo-De Beers. The Anglo-American Company provided De Beers with "technical services" such as mine managers, engineers, architects, bookkeepers, lawyers, and public relations advisers. They reported directly through a global telex system to a suite of offices on the fourth floor Of 44 Main Street, called simply "Diamond Services."

With the enormous profits from the diamond cartel, Oppenheimer built a mining conglomerate that operated on five continents. His father had invested heavily in gold mines in the Orange Free State, even though the price of gold was then fixed at $35 an ounce, and gold mining was unprofitable. As the price of gold rose, Oppenheimer expanded the gold mining until, in 1980s, his companies produced nearly one-third of all the gold produced in the world. As the gold mines in South Africa also yielded uranium oxide as a by-product, Oppenheimer also became one of the world's largest producers of uranium. Oppenheimer gradually expanded into platinum, copper, tin, manganese, oil, lead, zinc and other strategic minerals. By 1980s, his congeries of companies accounted for more than half of the value of South Africa's mineral and industrial exports. They also had international connections. For example, through Anglo-American Corporation he had become the second largest foreign investor in the United States in 1980s.

Oppenheimer was personally able to control this vast corporate complex, though he had only a small percent of the equity in it, through an ingeniously constructed pyramid of ownership. At the top of the pyramid was a private firm called E. Oppenheimer and Son. The chief shareholder in it were Harry Oppenheimer and his children. The principal asset of E. Oppenheimer and Son was ten percent of the shares of the Anglo-American Corporation. This block of stock was sufficient to give Oppenheimer undisputed control of it, since another 41 percent of the stock was held in the treasury of De Beers which was controlled by Oppenheimer.

At the next level of this complex structure, Anglo-American held a 52 percent interest in an investment trust called Anamint. Anamint, in turn, held 26 percent of the shares of De Beers -- a cross-holding that allowed Oppenheimer to appoint the board of directors of both companies.

The pyramid then dramatically widens with De Beers and Anglo-American owning pieces which when combined are tantamount to a controlling interest in seven of the largest conglomerates in South Africa. These investments, which included Anglo-American Gold Investment Company, Anglo-American Coal Corporation, and Johannesburg Consolidated Investment, encompassed most of the mining and industrial economy of South Africa: the companies, which themselves are holding companies, owned more than half of all the gold mines, the major insurance companies, the largest privately owned steel company in Africa, and virtually the entire petrochemical industry in South Africa. A government investigation of the holdings of the Oppenheimer Empire found that it exercised direct control over 900 major companies in South Africa.

Finally, at the base of the pyramid, Anglo-American controlled two international companies-Mineral and Resources Corporation in Bermuda and Charter Consolidated in Great Britain which together dominate mining companies on all five continents.

Because public investors owned stock in most of these corporations but did not exercise control, the pyramid structure permitted Oppenheimer to expand the reach of his empire without diminishing his personal hold over it. Because of this enormous leverage over these interlocking companies, he can act with swiftness and, if necessary, stealth, in acquiring new properties.

The financial holdings of the Anglo-De beers corporate pyramid provided the means for protecting the diamond invention in adverse times. Like pawns on a chess board, the swirl of corporations in the complex were used to safe guard the all-important queen in the game:

the diamond cartel.

Harry Oppenheimer groomed his only son Nicky to succeed him Educated at Harrow School and Christ Church, Oxford, where, like his father, he read Politics, Philosophy and Economics. Nicky joined the Anglo American Corporation in 1968 as the personal assistant to his father. And by 1981 he was appointed a member of the Executive Committee of the board of Anglo American Corporation and became Deputy Chairman in 1983. In 1985, he become Deputy Chairman of De Beers Consolidated Mines in 1985, when Harry Oppenheimer retired in 1998, Nicky Oppenheimer became Chairman of the De Beers Group.

Harry Oppenheimer died on August 19, 2000. By this time, the pyramid he had built to control the diamond empire had been lost in reorganizations necessary for financing its support of diamond prices. As more and more diamonds were discovered throughout the world, the cartel arrangement became less and less profitable. "Although it was a profitable AA+ company," an associate of Nicky Oppenheimer told me, "Its constant need to reinvest in the business left it with not much free cash."

De Beers also had been the target of anti-trust actions by both the United States and European Union. US prosecutors had pursued the diamond cartel ever since the nineteen-forties., alleging that it violated the Sherman Antitrust Act of 1890, which made it a crime to harm competition. To avoid criminal prosecution, De Beers's executives had to avoid traveling to the United States and maintain that they did not do business in the United States, which was by far the largest consumer of the company's diamonds. To maintain this fiction, De Beers had used a maze of supposedly-independent corporate entities, brokers, and diamond cutters. But while it was able to evade prosecuting for six decades, it was also unable to use the De Beers brand to directly participate in the highly-profitable retail jewelry business. So in October 2005, De Beers agreed to a preliminary agreement to settle the legal actions against it by returning $295 million to purchasers of its diamonds and consenting to an injunction prohibiting it from monopolizing the world supply of rough diamonds and from manipulating the price of polished diamonds. On May 27, 2008, the court, which would monitor De Beer's compliance, granted final approval of the settlement. De Beers also moved to head off a European Union investigation by transferring the stockpiling function of the cartel to

Alrosa, a Russian company, which, since it was based in Moscow, was free from the rules of the European Union.

Meanwhile, after each corporate reorganization, the Oppenheimer family holdings were decreased. By 2011, it amounted to only two percent. Nicky Oppenheimer's sway over the company had also diminished to the extent that he was not able to persuade the Anglo American board to appoint his only child, Jonathan Oppenheimer, replace him on the board. November 2011, Sir John Parker, the chairman of Anglo-American, offered him $5.1 billion dollars for the remaining Oppenheimer family's stake in De Beers. Nicky Oppenheimer accepted the offer, ending the Oppenheimers' century-long dominance of the diamond invention. A London banker involved in the finances of the cartel for three decades, observed. "Dynasty builders always end up face down in the snow."

Author's Note

Portions of this book appeared in *The Atlantic, Sunday Times of London, Wall Street Journal*, and the *International Herald Tribune*. Other parts of this book been drawn from my previous book, *The Rise and Fall of Diamonds*.

I am deeply thankful to Marjorie Kaplan and Rebecca Fraser for their research assistance and Bob Asahina, Harold Kaplan, Anne Jolis, and Bill Whitworth for their editing assistance.

I am also deeply grateful to Ben Bonas, Hugh Dagnell, William Goldberg, Richard Hambro, Barry Hawthorne, Albert Jolis, Jack Jolis, Peter J. R. Leyden, Barry R. Mortimer, Vivian Prince, Michael Samuels, Ivor Sanders, Bruno Schachner. Xan Smiley, Maurice Tempelsman, Richard Wake-Walker, and Ronald Winston for the insights they provided into the diamond trade.

About The Author

Edward Jay Epstein is the author of 15 books, and which have been excerpted in the *New Yorker, Atlantic,* and *Sunday Times of London*. He studied government at Cornell and Harvard, and received a PhD from Harvard. His master's thesis on the search for political truth became the best-selling *Inquest: The Warren Commission and the Establishment of Truth*. His doctoral dissertation on television news was published as *News From Nowhere*. He is the recipient of numerous of foundation grants and awards, including the prestigious Financial Times - Booz Allen prize for both best biography and best business book for *Dossier: The Secret History of Armand Hammer*.

His website is at www.edwardjayepstein.com

OTHER BOOKS BY EDWARD JAY EPSTEIN

Inquest
Legend
News From Nowhere
The Rise and Fall of Diamonds
Agency of Fear
Between Fact and Fiction
The Assassination Chronicles
Dossier: Armand Hammer
The Big Picture
The Hollywood Economist
Annals of Unsolved Crime

SHORT-FORM BOOKS

The JFK Assassination Diary
Sixty Version of the Kennedy Assassination
Three Days in May: The DSK Thriller
Myths of the Media
Armand Hammer: The Darker Side
The Rockefellers
Garrison's Game
Zia's Crash
Who Killed God's Banker
The Crude Cartel
Tabloid America: Crimes of the Press
The Money Demons: True Fables of Wall Street

66212872R00057

Made in the USA
Middletown, DE
09 March 2018